From a QUESTION *2 an* ANSWER

Memoirs of

Gary (Lovable) Summers

FriesenPress

Suite 300 - 990 Fort St
Victoria, BC, V8V 3K2
Canada

www.friesenpress.com

First Edition — 2020

Editing by FriesenPress

ISBN
978-1-5255-8293-6 (Hardcover)
978-1-5255-8292-9 (Paperback)
978-1-5255-8294-3 (eBook)

1. FAMILY & RELATIONSHIPS, DEATH, GRIEF, BEREAVEMENT

Distributed to the trade by The Ingram Book Company

Table of Contents

INTRODUCTION

IF MY MEMORY serves me correctly, it was early September of 1963, I was young, carefree and somewhat spoiled, and because of these reasons, I was dreading my impending task. Intriguing? Not really. It was just the opposite. I was on my way to an elderly woman's home (she was probably about forty something at the time) anyway; my father had volunteered my services, and I was to clean, caulk and prepare her storm windows. The elderly woman, whom I had just met the day before at a social gathering, was a relative of my father's, 'lady friend,'-ok; it was his girl friend, Elvira. I was eighteen years old at the time, and had recently lost my mother to cancer. I was about to enter the U.S. Navy and was staying at Elvira's home in the interim. (My father did not shack up with Elvira at the time, which made their relationship seem, more proper and acceptable, especially to me.)

Getting back to the elder woman, and the more I think about it, she was probably 35ish. She seemed very lofty in her views concerning life, and all things pertaining. She asked me what I was going to do with my life. She asked me what my strengths were. She asked me so many questions that I was somewhat embarrassed, because I really didn't have any concrete answers. I had never established any goals in my life. I had dreams and fantasies (I was quite a dreamer) but I had never really thought seriously about long-term goals, or my future (other than wanting a higher education, and some kind of status in life). I wanted to make everyone in my family proud of me, especially my father.

Getting back to the-less elderly woman.... During a conversation, she conveyed to me, that I had a special talent, in that I was able to communicate very well. I felt very proud at that moment, for I had a new-found talent. I then blurted out to her that I had always thought of writing a book. She encouraged me further, and asked what it would be about. I said, "It would be about life and death."

Why not? I thought. I knew so much about the subject because; I was eighteen years old and had experienced it all. I had all the answers. She pressed further. "What will you title your book? Without hesitation I said, **"From a Question to an Answer."**

CHAPTER 1

From A Question

MY MOTHER'S DEATH was most unbearable, and right from the moment that she was diagnosed with this disgusting disease, I pondered deeply as to why such a young, beautiful, loving, thoughtful, caring person, would have to be subjected to the horrible pain and suffering that she would have to endure. Not only did she endure, she endured with strength, pride, humor and courage. My mother's main concern at the time, however, was not for herself, but for me, and what would become of me.*

During the weeks, days, minutes and even the seconds leading up to my mother's death, she was not in an unconscious state, but yet, she was not conscious of her surroundings, and not conscious of what she was saying. What she did say though, during this time, was so profoundly 'amazing' and so 'unworldly', that my *Question* as to, what my mother's purpose in life was, and why she had to die so prematurely, started to emerge and would become, over a period of several years, an *Answer.*

***I would like to qualify this statement by adding that, at the time of my mothers' diagnosis, I was only 17 years old. My sister, five years my senior and at least twenty years wiser, was pretty well established to continue on in life. She was a registered nurse, and had carefully selected the man that she was going to marry. They did, and they still are.**

My father and mother had been estranged from each other for a period of time before her diagnosis, but they were still morally and caringly bonded.

*I, on the other hand, was spoiled, pampered, and at that time, I was just starting to become 'Lovable'. ***

Some years before, my mother had once called me her best pal, but she probably and without my knowing, called my sister her best pal many times more often. I was only in grade ten and didn't really have a mature outlook about life. I truly believe that in my mothers mind, she could not fathom any idea of what was going to happen to me, and took this concern to her grave.

***Later, in years to come, my wife called me 'Lovable' quite often. Not as a term of endearment however, but just the opposite. It was to point out to me that I was being obnoxious. My wife very rarely says anything bad about anyone and she seldom uses derogatory words. If she did, she would have called me what 'Lovable' really meant: 'Asshole'*

My mom, Helen Pauline Summers nee Hilborn at the age of 46 just before being diagnosed with cancer.

Lovable

FEBRUARY 9, 1945 was a very special occasion for me and I only realize this in hindsight because I can't remember a single thing about it. It was the day that I, Gary Howard Summers was born.

I came into the world at the Hotel Dieu Hospital in Windsor Ontario Canada, the proud son of, Helen Pauline (nee Hilborn) and Alexander Daniel Summers. As I learned later in life, my 5-year-old sister, Beverly Ann wasn't too happy with the idea of having a little brother. She didn't like me at all, and would have preferred that I went back to wherever it was that I had come from. Why would she want to be rid of me anyway? I was so 'Lovable' and I would become even more 'Lovable' as time went on. So much so, that I could understand her wanting to be rid of me later in my life, but not in February of 1945.

If I were to dedicate a page(s) in this book to acknowledge a particular person, for unknowingly contributing to my becoming less 'Lovable' and list all of the positive outcomes that resulted from our brief encounter, it would probably set a record for the longest dedication in the history of literature. (Not that I am a *literaturist*, nor do I ever expect to be one.) And there probably isn't even a word like that in the dictionary, although there should be. So I will simply include his contribution with an elaborate explanation as follows:

1965

MY SHIP WAS docked at the naval base in Norfolk Virginia, and after a shore leave I returned aboard. I found a subordinate, asleep at the watch. Although I was a lovable person, I occasionally became more lovable, so much so that I woke him up and belted him, right in the face. It was a cowardly sucker punch, and it made me feel sick to my stomach, and I thought "How could I do such a thing"? But having some kind of stupid pride, I did not apologize, and stubbornly maintained my evil decorum. The duty officer was called and I was immediately confined to the ship until further notice. The further notice would be by means of a formal disciplinary review.

I felt bad, but in more ways than one. I was about to go on a 72-hour shore leave beginning the next morning. Myself, and three of my friends were to head north for the weekend. My buddy Sandy had a car and would drop Ted off in Pittsburgh, Barry in Toledo, myself in Detroit and then Sandy would continue on his way to northern Michigan. We had previously arranged the timing and our pick up points for our return to Norfolk.

That night as I sulked and pouted over my despair, I made a decision that would ultimately have quite an impact on my life. I would simply, 'jump ship.'

The next morning, into my civvies and against the advice of my friends, I 'jumped ship' and ventured home. My ultimate destination: Windsor Ontario, Canada. I couldn't wait to get there, but little did I know that my arrival would be delayed, and eight hours of my shore leave would be spent in a Monroe Michigan jail cell.

After dropping off Ted, we soon reached Toledo and drove Barry to his destination. It wasn't his home, but a bar that he was well acquainted with and where his high school crush was waiting for him. Her name was Kay and I remember that name very well because the joke on board our ship, relating to Berry, was the word FUCK. It was vulgar, and I very seldom use vulgar words but it meant, 'If you see Kay' while in Toledo, "send her my love."

We had a few beers with Barry and Kay, and, maybe a few more before we finally bade farewell. I can still picture that moment when they left the bar. Kay was driving a brand-new Mustang convertible, and Barry, with a grin that reached both of his ears waved goodbye. At that moment I was so envious of Barry and I thought to myself, that he had the whole world in the palm of his hand.

Sandy and I returned to the bar for one more drink, and bought a case of beer to go. We were on our way north, free as a bird, but our next stop, however, would be at a magistrate's court in Monroe Michigan.

Not guilty your honour, I pleaded, as I stood facing a very stern, authoritive and miserable looking figure. He was wearing the customary black robe of a magistrate but he probably had his pyjamas on underneath because it was three o'clock in the morning, and the police had just woke him up to attend this kangaroo court. I was pleading not guilty to the outlandish charges against me. Sandy entered the same plea. The only difference being, he was guilty. I wasn't.

Earlier, when we had left the bar in Toledo en route to Michigan, we were pulled over by a state trooper. I said to Sandy "quick! Get out of the car and open the hood, we'll make out like we have car trouble". When the trooper approached I asked him politely if I could use his flashlight, which he handed to me.

While we searched around the engine compartment for the unknown, the trooper walked around the car. Upon returning to the front of the car he asked if we found the problem and I said that we had, it was a loose wire or something like that. He said that he noticed a case of beer on the front seat. I explained that we weren't impaired but just having a few beers on our long journey to stay awake. I see he said, "Let's check out the vehicle." He told Sandy to open the drivers' door, and after having a look inside he told him to “close it.” I don’t know what got in to Sandy but he slammed the door shut. The trooper cautioned him to “take it easy.” He then asked Sandy to open the trunk, and again he said, “Close it” and again Sandy slammed it shut. “Cool it” I whispered. The trooper opened the passenger side door and then opened the glove compartment. “Close it” he said and once again Sandy slammed it shut. The writing was on the wall. “I’m taking you two in, and we’ll have a little talk with the magistrate.” Obviously not being judged as impaired (I’m not really sure that we weren’t) we were told to followed him in Sandy’s’ car to the Magistrates office. The charge was drinking while driving and we were found guilty. We were ordered to pay a hefty fine, or serve six days in jail in lieu of the fine. We, in no way, had enough money to pay the fine, so off to jail we went. Behind bars? Lovable me? What a miscarriage of justice. What I was about to experience, however, gave me a lesson that I would never forget.

The prison guard cordially greeted us when we entered the doors of Alcatraz, which up until then I thought Alcatraz was near San

Francisco but it's not, it's in Monroe Michigan. He was, to me, a lumbering giant but he always wore a friendly smile. He asked me what I did for a living and I replied to him that I was in the navy, stationed in Norfolk Virginia. Still wearing a smile, he, not so politely, grabbed me by my jacket lapels and lifted me up above his head level and slammed me into a stone wall. His explanation was; he was in the Marines and despised 'Swabs' "I will make sure you enjoy your stay here," he said.

Sandy and I were thrown, literally, into the 'drunk tank'. When I awoke the next morning, I faced the hardest group of people that I have ever seen. I asked the guy next to me what he was in for. "I shot somebody," he said, while he pointed his hand and finger as an imaginary gun. *Let me out of here!* I thought. My other companions, okay cellmates, and their stories didn't perk up my spirits much either

Sandy and I were summoned, and we were taken out of the 'drunk-tank.' At last, I thought, only to find out that we were about to be issued prison uniforms, and that we would be transferred to a semi-permanent cell. Oh! My Gosh! I said to myself.

When I asked permission for Sandy and me to make some phone calls in order to get money to pay our fine, we were told that we were each allowed two calls. Reverse charges only! I phoned my best friend in Windsor Ontario, and after hearing my plea, he hung up. Why? I thought. I phoned my father as my last resort. He hung up. Why? I thought. Sandy didn't want to involve his family so he called Barry in Toledo. Good move. His sister answered and said that Barry was hung over and didn't want to talk, but she would come to our rescue. Relief at last!

Barry's sister and her husband arrived a couple of hours later to pay our fine and bail us out of this mess. I was so, so, happy, and so, so, relieved. We were free! I cannot remember how, or even if we paid Barry's sister back, but I'm sure we did because if we didn't, our ass would grass and Barry would be the lawn mower.

Sandy and I got ready to resume our trip north. Sandy's first stop was a beer store, and yes, he bought a case of Blue Ribbon Beer. We were on our way again and Sandy said, "have a beer Gary let's celebrate." "There is nothing to celebrate Sandy; I'm in deep shit when we get back to the ship. I'm in deep shit when and if, I get home and face my father. I'm in deep shit all around and I feel like shit; so don't even talk to me." Things were very quiet until we were about a half an hour away from Detroit and my drop off spot. It was probably about noon and I said "what the hell, I'll have a beer." After a couple of gulps I started to feel better and we talked about my pick up point on Sunday morning. Sandy let me off, and I hitch hiked my way to the Detroit –Windsor Tunnel.

Home at last, but nobody was home. Of course no one was expecting me because I didn't tell them I was coming. Oh well. I went to my father's local watering hole, the Royal Tavern on Wyandotte street and had a few beers. My dad finally arrived, and because of the look on his face, I didn't know if he was totally shocked to see me, if he was disappointed to see me, or it was too sudden a surprise, but he warmly greeted me and introduced me to his cronies. The beer flowed, and what we did the rest of the night is somewhat a blur to me.

I don't remember if I saw my sister and brother-law that night but I really believe that my father and I bonded. I also think that it was the first time that I drank with my father because I had always said to him that I would never drink alcohol, and he used to say, "Never say never Gary." How right he was.

Little did I know, however, that the previously mentioned contributor to my becoming less 'Lovable' was about to come on the scene, and greatly impact my direction in life.

A Change in Direction

I LEFT WINDSOR early Sunday morning and hitched rides to my pick up point on the outskirts of Detroit. I arrived at my pick up point a few hours early. No surprise though, I am always early, I have always been early, and probably always will be early. I sometimes feel that I was born nine months premature. With a lot of time to put in, and having little money, I basically roamed around the area, moping, feeling sorry for myself, and worrying about what was going to happen to me when I returned to my ship. I had a very heavy heart. (What a spoiled suck I was) At some point I went into a convenience store just to browse around and put in a little time when a local customer approached me. He made a comment that I looked lost and wondered if everything was okay. I explained to him that I was in the navy, based in Norfolk Virginia and that I was waiting for a shipmate to pick me up on the corner just outside the store and we would then return to our ship after a weekend leave. Details are somewhat sketchy on what he actually said, but he had a totally relaxing and trusting demeanour about him. He offered to take me to his home a couple of blocks away, meet his family, have a bite to eat, and he would return me to the corner on time. I accepted.

His home was beautiful and his family welcomed me warmly. Given my present circumstances, they made me feel very comfortable and relaxed. While his wife made lunch he led me to his library room. It was a huge room but it had a cozy like den atmosphere. He introduced me to some of his favourite books, favourite authors, and how their writings had influenced his life. Motivational, religious, historical and classical works; it was a library collection that put me in awe. Within a short period of time I was in awe with him as well.

He explained to me that he was a self-made man and that he was now enjoying the fruits of his labour: he has a successful business with a close knit, happy family, and, at this point in his life, he had contentment. But more importantly to me, and hitting closer to home, was his story of troubled times and hardships which all stemmed from him being too immature early in his adult life. He had energy and he had potential but it was all misdirected. What was the turning point in his life? Simply put, a woman, who was now his wife and best friend.

He went on to explain how he achieved, "positive thinking, setting achievable goals and most importantly.... Learning from others through reading and listening" I was listening!

He returned me to my pick up point on time, and I thanked him for all he had done for me. I didn't realize at the time how much he had really done for me but it would soon start to sink in and would make a positive change to the direction of my life. I have but one regret about our encounter, I did not get his address, and due to my troubled state of mind, I had much too quickly forgotten his name.

Sandy arrived on time, and we headed to Toledo and then on to Pittsburgh to pick up Barry and Ted. During the ride back to Norfolk I wasn't my usual yapping self; instead, I pondered and reflected as to what had just transpired during the past three days. Most of my thoughts reflected back to my newly found mentor in his 'library.' His thoughts and words consumed me.

"Positive thinking and setting realistic goals" my mentor had said. I had always thought that I was a positive person, but maybe my thinking was; that I was 'always positively right, and all others were positively wrong.' My idea of setting goals was realistic, however, the goals I would set were very short term, and very shallow. Like, 'starting tomorrow I'm going to stop borrowing money from the slush fund'. I would stop, but it would only last a couple of days and I would again be borrowing from the slush fund. For this privilege, I would end up having to pay a whopping 40% interest come the next payday. It got to the point where I would go through the pay line, and continue through the next hatch to give most of my pay to the slush funder.

My other thoughts centred on what was going to happen in a few hours when I reported on board my ship. Would I be arrested and thrown in the brig. Would I be court marshalled, and be demoted? Woe is me! One thing was for sure; I was going to turn my life around.

We arrived at the Norfolk naval base late that night. As I boarded my ship and with great apprehension, I was relieved to find out that there was no mention of me being AWOL. After boarding, I went below decks were I was greeted by a friend of mine. He informed me that my crew covered for me while I was AWOL and that the 'Officer of the Day' who had put me on charge and confined me to the ship, had been on a 72 hour pass him-self. Whew!!!!! I still had to face a tribunal the next day but that seemed minor at this moment. I slept well.

Before the mast

"SUMMERS REPORT TO the Executive Officer immediately" Was this anyway to be greeted on a Monday morning? How rude! Oh, I forgot for a moment that I was going to become less lovable. Wow, this was going to take some work.

Nervously I tapped gently on the X.O.'s door and was greeted with a not-so-warm 'Enter!' Upon entering I responded "Summers reporting as requested Sir." I was not asked to take a seat, nor was I told to stand at ease. The X.O. explained that I was charged with a very serious offence and asked me to explain my actions. If I hadn't met my 'mentor' the previous day I would have been very defensive in my explanation, but after hours of pondering and reflecting I replied that "I had over stepped my limited authority and that I could not defend my actions. What I did was wrong and cowardly of me." With that he stood up and looked me straight in the eyes and said, "What you did Summers was not only wrong it was inhumane. Do you have any idea how that seaman, which you cowardly smashed in the face, feels? Have you given any thought to the humiliation, not to mention, the pain that you inflicted upon him?" Without allowing me to respond he said, "One more question Summers." "Have you apologized to him?" "No Sir, I haven't had the opportunity but I will, I promise." The X.O. replied, "You haven't had the opportunity, and yet you have been confined to this ship for three days?" The X.O.'s nose was only a gap away from mine, and his eyes where glaring when he said, "you are not only a coward, who needs a lesson in humanity, but you are also a liar. Get out of my quarters immediately. I will pass judgement on you at my convenience. Until then you will continue to be restricted to the ship. Do you understand?" I replied, "Yes sir and I am sorry Sir! I will never do anything like this again." I immediately exited and thought to myself that there was so much more I wanted to say to him, not for the reason of reducing my sentence, but to ensure him that I am in the process of changing my ways, and at that moment, I wanted him to like me, and to believe in me.

Still flaunting my stubborn pride I was trying to choose a good time to confront the seaman. I didn't want anyone around when I apologized to him because that would show a weakness. I did, however, sincerely want to apologize. I actually wanted to say I was sorry immediately after I hit him but it was that stupid stubborn pride.

My opportunity came when he was going on watch and he was just closing his locker. He didn't see me coming when I approached him and when I called his name I thought he was going to go into shock. He turned chalk white. To alleviate any fears that he might have had, thinking that I might be coming to retaliate because I was put on report, I quickly said that I was sorry for what I had done. I offered my hand in hope that he would offer his, so that we could shake and put this behind us. We did shake, and I actually believe that we shared the same emotion at that moment. I felt a little mist in my eye and I think he did as well. To relieve this awkward moment I asked if he was going on watch to which he replied that he was. I said that I would check on him later to make sure that he wasn't sleeping. He grinned and our tension was over. More importantly for me, I felt like a heavy load of chips was just lifted from my shoulders. I felt good.

I don't remember how long it was before I was summonsed to see the X.O. but it seemed like a long time. It was probably a deliberate delay so I could stew over my impending punishment but I wasn't stewing, I was ready for anything no matter how harsh the penalty because I deserved it and, I was actually looking forward to judgement day. Was I starting to grow up?

The day of judgement came and upon entering the X.O.'s quarters I felt a different atmosphere compared to my first encounter. "Summers reporting as requested sir." The X.O. told me to have a seat. "Have you been keeping your nose out of trouble lately Summers?" "Yes sir." I replied "and, I did apologize to the seaman sir." "I know" he said, he told me. I had called him in to find out what his feelings where as to what punishment best suited the charge against you." "He also told me that you had invited him ashore for some beers when your restriction was lifted." I believe you told him that it might be weeks but it was okay because you would be able to save up enough money for a good piss up. Is that right? He asked with a smile. Smiling back I said, "Yes sir." "Well Summers I think you'll be able to go for a 'little' piss up sooner than that. I have talked with your CPO, and the Engineering Officer; both had some positive things to say about your performance. Your chief did say that you were a little rough around the edges and needed a little filing down from time to time but overall you're okay." "Thank you sir," I said. The X.O. continued, "I have weighed this situation carefully and have arrived at the following decision."

"You are no longer confined to the ship but you will perform two hours of extra duty each day for seven days. Your chief will give you a duty list of what he wants done and you will carry them out on your honour, without supervision, and report back to me in a week's time explaining what you had accomplished. Dismissed!" As I stood up I said "Thank you sir," and I thought to myself, I think he likes me! I think he likes me! Yahoo!

While performing my extra duties, I had a lot of private time to think about things. I got off very lightly from a very serious charge. Why? And why did I get away with being AWOL? What had brought me to my 'mentor' and at such a crucial time? With each question came more questions. I reviewed my life and started to think that I was being led somewhere, that I was not in total control of my destiny. I also felt, as most people probably feel, that I was special, but I also felt that I was better than everyone else. What an inflated ego! But it's true; I have felt that way most of my life. I reflected over the past two years of all the good things that have happened to me, and all the bad things that could have happened to me but didn't. Here I was in the U.S. Navy. Why? The answer was simple enough but I hadn't taken the time to even consider the question before or even think about it. I was having too much fun and living as carefree as possible under the constraints of military discipline. Boy did I need that discipline!

I wondered where I would be if my mother were still living. I probably wouldn't be here in the navy, but now I was, Of course! It's my mom!

Not that her passing away was the reason I'm here, and of course it is, but I started to get a sensation that she didn't pass far away. She was here and always has been. Of course! There's no doubt. She is here and she's looking out for me. Everything started to fall in place, and my recent life started to make sense. A profound feeling came over me, it was like an aura that surrounded me and I began to pray and I have prayed every day since.

I completed my seven days of extra duty, and completed my duties above and beyond the call of extra duty. I must admit that being lovable or not, I have always been a good worker and it got to a point later in my life were I became a workaholic. I carried out my duties just as the X.O. said it would be done, on my honour and without supervision.

My CPO never checked on my progress other than asking me how my work was going. Maybe he had checked, now and again, but it wasn't apparent to me. Possibly, and thinking about it later, it was probably the X.O. that gave instructions to give me full rein, in order for him to determine my integrity.

It was the day after I completed my extra duty that I asked permission to approach the X.O. With permission granted, I was invited to his quarters and was asked to sit down. As requested, I explained to him my extra duty accomplishments and tried to impress upon him that I did a good job. He knew I did a good job, because the chief had told him. He explained to me that I was not spied on during the past week but he had originally asked my CPO to make an inspection of my work areas at the end of my 'sentence.' He explained that my CPO was more than pleased with my work and that I had now paid my debt. He further explained that the charge against me would not be entered in my file and that I still had a chance to earn a good conduct medal. Boy, I thought, they have medals for everything.

Before being dismissed, the X.O. asked if I had learned anything positive from this experience. I quickly responded, "Yes Sir, and thank you! Sir." I wanted to add more detail but it just wouldn't come out. As I reached the door, I heard the X.O. say, "Keep your promise to the seaman Summers, and go have a few beers, but don't you get pissed, okay?" I replied with a smile, "I'll keep my promise Sir and won't get pissed, but he might!" It turned out that I lied again. Dam! We did go for some beers, and I did pay, but I got pissed, he didn't. I learned a lot that night. I had always thought of him as some sort of wimp but as I discovered, he was stronger than me in many ways. We became fairly good friends and to this day, I shudder to think what I did to him by giving him that cowardly sucker punch.

My life did change for the better and during the next two years, besides seeing most of the world and crossing the equator to become a Shellback, I also crossed the Arctic Circle to become a Blue nose. I read a lot, and learned a lot. I received my High School diploma through GED exams with an 85% average. I took various correspondence courses ranging from economics to mathematics. Most of the reading materials that I enjoyed, and still do, is non-fiction or at least based on fact, and I especially enjoy history and biographies.

Closing in on the end of my enlistment, I had applied for entrance at two colleges. I even took a college entrance exam under the auspices of a Commissioned Officer. I passed my exam and was elated, but more profoundly, I was proud! I was accepted by either East Tennessee State University or Kent State in Ohio, I cannot remember which college it was because another, more positive, 'mother, influence' would lead me back to Canada after my discharge.

The USS Valcour changed its designation from AVP 55 to AGF I and was the flag ship for the Commander Middle East force Rear Admiral J. H. Maurer.

CHAPTER 2

The USS VALCOUR

The Middle East

HOWEVER, IN THE mean time before completing my four-year stint in the USN, I was actually settling into navy life, and to a degree I was enjoying it. I was on my second, one-year rotation in the Middle East. I was aboard the (*USS Valcour AGF I)* which was recently converted from AVP 55. It was painted white and was nicknamed, 'The White Ghost of the Persian Gulf.' Actually, it was the flag Ship of the, Commander of the Middle East Force. The electronic communications systems aboard were very high tech and, were state of the art. Security was tight, so much so that being a Canadian; I didn't have a high enough security clearance to enter the communications room. At the time, I was the P.O. in charge of the electrical section and I wasn't even allowed to go into the communications room to assist, or even check on any of my crew working in there. Personally I think the Valcour was on a spy mission.

On my first tour in the Middle East, a year and a half prior, I was in my early days of being 'Lovable' and had my first opportunity to meet and talk to an Admiral. The ship was anchored outside of Bahrain and I was working alone on the bridge, trouble-shooting an electrical circuit when a voice behind me ask what I was doing. The voice sounded familiar, so thinking it was a mate of mine, I replied, "What the fuck does it look like I'm doing?" The voice replied, "I only asked." I turned around and there he was, the Admiral, the Commander of the Middle East Force. I was in total shock but I think I blurted out something like, "I, I, I'm sorry Sir. I didn't realize that you were a Sir, I mean an Admiral. I, I mean, I'm sorry Admiral!" He replied something like, "Don't worry about it. It was just small talk anyway, carry on." What a guy! What an Admiral! I loved that guy. I mean. I loved that 'Sir.' After changing my underwear, I completed my work on the bridge.

"Thanks mom! I guess you were there as well, but at least you didn't have to change my diapers this time. I did it all by myself."

My second tour of duty in the gulf was a little different from the first. We headed further east this time, and were nearing an area of serious conflict, a conflict that was quickly escalating, 'Vietnam.'

Vietnam

AS THE CONFLICT in Vietnam grew, many Americans were beginning to question their country's role in the involvement. More and more troupes were being deployed, and more and more troupes were being killed. I had very limited knowledge of the situation, being at sea; we received very little international news.

All I knew; I was serving in the armed forces of the United States, my adopted country and 'we' were at war. I had heard that many young Americans were dodging the draft and fleeing to Canada. This bothered me at the time. I viewed these draft dodgers as cowards, deserters, wimps, and even traitors.

I was proud to be serving in the military of such a fine, and caring nation. I was proud of my uniform. I was proud of the Stars and Stripes. I was proud. I was brave, and I was also naïve, but at the time, I was going to do something about it.*

> ***Please keep in mind that this was in 1967. Unfortunately! At the time of this writing, I have drastically changed my personal views concerning the United States, especially their international involvement and the lack of their own national involvement.***

I made a formal requested to my Commanding Officer for a transfer to Vietnam. Via word of mouth, scuttlebutt, or whatever, I had heard about certain boats being used in Vietnam, similar to the PT boats used in WW2, and they were being used to patrolled the rivers and tributaries of Vietnam with the sole mission to, 'Seek and destroy the enemy!' I was told that these patrol boats engaged a crew of three marines, a mechanic and an electrician. I envisioned being that electrician.

My request for transfer was denied. The reason? I was the senior Petty Officer of the electrical section and at in this stage of our deployment, there was no one qualified to replacement me. Of course I felt proud to hear that I was irreplaceable, but I thought, "What was the C.O. thinking?" Americans were dodging the draft and heading to Canada every day. I was a Canadian volunteering to risk my life on behalf of 'America.' I was just beginning to be 'Less Lovable' but there is a limit as to how less lovable you can be.

When I was talking about this situation with my mates, someone suggested that I write my senator or congressman. "I don't have a senator or congressman, I'm a Canadian." Then I heard someone say, "Use mine, I don't use him." Bingo!

I wrote a letter to Senator Young of Ohio. I explained my situation in detail and that my request for a transfer to Vietnam was denied. He simply, but cordially, replied that he would look into it. It wasn't long before I received correspondence from high-level navy brass indicating that they were looking into to the situation. The bottom line, of the final communiqué was, "If I ship over, and extend my enlistment, my transfer would be approved."

Well what do you think of that? Here I am, willing to shed my blood for the cause, and the navy wants another pound of my flesh. All of my heroic and patriotic fantasies were put to rest. I was offering enough as it was. I wasn't going to offer more.

Later, while pondering this current state of affairs, I thought that I could have ended up being sent home in a box, and even a powerful 'spiritual being' couldn't stop a bullet being fired at me, but, a powerful 'spiritual being' could very well stop my request for a transfer. Thanks again mom!

Something very shocking happened to me a short time later. I received transfer orders. I was to return stateside ASAP and report aboard the *U.S.S. Recovery*. What the hell was going on? I couldn't be replaced a few weeks ago but now I was being transferred? It didn't take long for it to sink in however, and I learned another valuable lesson. 'Do not! Ever! Go over the head of your Commanding Officer, and especially, over his head to a U.S. Senator.'

Me manning the Electrical Switchboard during Battle Stations drill.

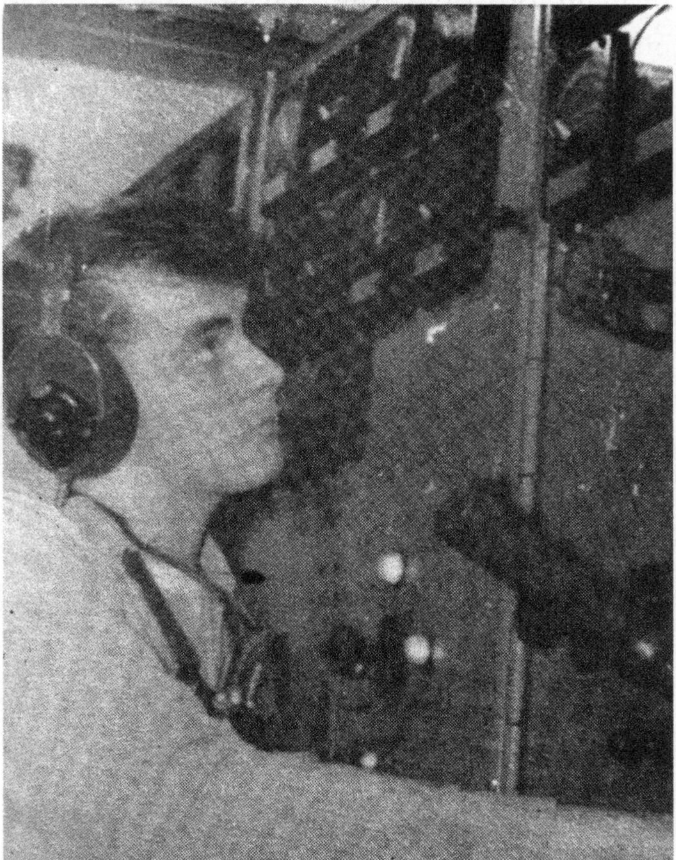

Farewell 'Valcour'

WITHIN A SHORT period of time I was ready to go, and I was looking good! Not being allowed to fly in uniform, for whatever reason, I was decked out in my black Mohair suit that I had purchased just a few weeks ago. On my first tour of duty in the Gulf I learned that many sailors and officers purchased clothing from 'Mohammad the Tailor' on the island of Bahrain. I had no reason at the time to visit Mohammed because I had a uniform and there was nothing in the near future that would require me to wear civilian clothes. On this voyage however, I had a reason, I was becoming a short timer and had less than a nine months to serve in the navy. Besides my Mohair suit, I purchased a white trench coat, two sport coats, one red and one blue, plus two pairs of black slacks. Each jacket was lined with silver coloured silk, and the inside pocket was embroidered with Mohammad's internationally famous signature.

The time frame between my flight out of the Middle East and the date that I was required to report aboard the (*USS Recovery*) allowed me to take a one-week leave. I would spend this time in my hometown, Windsor, Ontario Canada.

The evening that I left the *'Valcour'* I had mixed emotions. I was pumped up, but at the same time, I was pumped down. I have always hated goodbyes and I still do, mainly because I am such an emotional suck. I didn't want any fanfare. No hugs. No tears. The timing for my departure was perfect because the evening movie was just beginning and it was being shown on the fantail. This allowed me to leave quietly from my floating sanctuary where I had lived for close to three years. I headed for the airport with a heart heavier than my luggage.

Once on board my plane I had to acclimatize myself to this strange group of people that I was travelling with. They were civilians. I had to restrain myself from telling the person across the aisle from me that his shoes needed shinning and to "Give me twenty push ups!" It was time to start to relax, become less 'Lovable' and celebrate my return home. I did celebrate, and after a brief stopover in Cairo, and Athens, we arrived in Rome. Passengers that were continuing en-route to the U.S. had to disembark and transfer planes. I happened to be first in line at the exit and as I stepped off the plane; I missed my first step and simply rolled down the portable stairs like a black Mohair snowball to the bottom, and onto the tarmac.

Besides being embarrassed, my first thought was 'they should warn passengers, that at 30,000 miles in the air, you might not feel the effects of alcohol, but you certainly will feel the effects when you land.' I also and vividly remember the stewardess who came running post-haste down the stairs to see if I was okay, I had happened to be laying in the perfect position to see all the way up her dress, so wearing a smile I simply replied, "Thank you stewardess, I'm okay now.

I don't remember too much about the next leg of my journey bound for N.Y. City because I think I slept through most of it. I do remember hitting it off quite well with a stewardess. We were getting close to our arrival time when she handed me a note containing her full name and telephone number and said, "If you're ever in the area, give me a call." I thought to myself, "Do I really have to go home?"

After arriving in Detroit and taking a bus through the Detroit/Windsor tunnel, I was home again. I looked at my watch and was stunned to realise that with the distance that I had travelled, and taking into consideration the time changes, I had arrived home exactly on the same day and about the same time that I had left the Middle East the day before.

I immediately went to the Royal Tavern to see my father. I knew he would be there because he was now renting an apartment upstairs. His 'lady friend' Elvira, was now a distant memory. How convenient it was for someone who enjoyed drinking draft beer to simply walk down a flight stairs and step up to the bar. He was there all right and he happily greeted me, but he was obviously not overly proud to see me. Who would? I can imagine how unkempt I looked. A twenty-four hour beard growth, a supposedly white coloured shirt that was now turning a bit brownish, wearing a black Mohair suit that looked as though I had slept in a gutter with it.

This was not the image I wanted to portray to my father because I was now more mature, and somewhat more refined, better read, and

I wanted him to be proud of me because I was turning out to be good 'Summers' stock. It was okay though; I had a whole week ahead to substantiate my progression up the ladder of the human race.

The next day my father asked if I wanted to shoot some pool. It took me by surprise because I have never known him to play the game. I asked, "You shoot pool?" He replied, "I have been known to play on occasion." Off we went to the pool hall. After easily beating him on the first game, he asked if I wanted to make it more interesting. "Sure what do you have in mind?" Well he said, "The loser of the next game buys dinner for four after you get out of the navy." "You're on!" I said, and thought to myself "what a sucker my dad is, here I am a seasoned sailor, a world traveller, who has spent many hours playing pool while on shore leaves, and his only claim was to have been known to play 'on occasion?" "Rack them up dad!" It was my break, and feeling comfortable after putting a couple of balls in the pocket, it was my dad's turn. He ran the table! After the eight ball dropped in, he smiled and said, "Dinner for four Gary." I was totally in disbelief; I was hustled by my own father.

About two nights later, standing at the bar of the 'Royal Tavern' we were putting back some draft beer and I was trying to impress my dad and his friends with my ability to hold liqueur. I ordered a shot of cherry brandy and chugged it back. I ordered another one later, and my dad simply said, "Take it easy Gary, don't overdo it." "No problem dad, I can handle it." Just a few moments later I turned to my dad to say something but words didn't come out, the only thing that came out was my vomit, and it spewed all over the front of my dad. Oh, my, gosh!

It was the most embarrassing thing that had ever happened to me in my life, and I am absolutely certain, that it was the most embarrassing thing that had ever happened to my dad, in his entire life! That's all I remember about that night.

The next morning I thought, "I am really impressing my dad with my progression up the ladder of the human race." At the same time I had a flash back to an event that happened only couple of years back. I was on leave, and my father was treating me to a steak dinner at the

'Riverside Yacht Club.' My dad wore a suit, and I was in my dress whites. The dining room at the yacht club was elegant, and I felt very privileged to be there. Although not having a yacht, my dad was a member and a regular patron. Dinner was served and I dug right in, literally, I dug right into my steak and I can remember it like it was yesterday, the plate flipped completely over and landed on my lap. I was so embarrassed that I felt like crying, and I think my father wanted to disown me.

For the last couple of days before my departure, I maintained a low profile and simply licked my wounds. My dad was very forgiving, he always had been, and I had never understood that. I did however understand later in life.

My leave, thank goodness, came to an end and back to Norfolk Virginia I was bound. This was going to be my last assignment in the USN, and I was looking forward to closing this chapter in my life. It would soon be time to move on to greater things, and move on I would.

The Valcour Revisited.

I REPORTED ABOARD the (*USS Discovery*) late at night. I found my rack and crashed. The next morning after revelry and pretending to still be asleep, I heard a couple people whispering when they realised that a newcomer was in the quarters. I felt comfortable when I heard one of them say, "Well he's not a green horn, he's a petty officer." They were obviously looking at my tunic, which I had laid on my duffle bag beside my rack. I have to admit that it was little unnerving to wake up in strange quarters and not know a single person, but it didn't take long for the curious to find out who I was.

After chow I met my superiors and divisional colleagues and was given a tour of the ship. The *'Recovery'* was a navy diving ship and was equipped with all the necessary equipment including a decompression chamber. It wasn't long before I found out that we would soon be underway, destination, the North Atlantic. Our mission at the time was unknown. Déjà vu.

I had an instant recall to an event that had happened in 1965, about a year and a half prior.

The *Valcour* was a 'rotational' flag Ship in the Middle East and was presently 'off duty.' One of her three sister ships, the *Greenwich Bay*, was now the flag ship "on duty." The third sister was the *Duxbury Bay*.

Obviously having too much time on her hands, the 'Valcour' was sent on a mission to the North Atlantic.

This North Atlantic assignment soon became a very intriguing and a very covert operation. Before shipping out, all of *Valour's* identifications were removed or painted over. During our mission there were strict regulations concerning refuse: all garbage had to be burnt on the fantail, and not even a single chewing gum wrapper could be tossed overboard.

We set sail and headed across the 'pond' once again. After many days at sea, and still not having a clue what was going on, we entered the English Channel, headed north, and then docked at the Rosyth shipyard, which is about ten minutes away from Edinburgh, Scotland. For whatever reason we were there, I did not know, but it was an enjoyable visit. I think we were in port for about three, pea-soup fog days. Back and forth, by taxi, each day to Edinburgh, we couldn't see anything surrounding us because of the fog, but on our final day the fog cleared, the sun shone and I was blown away by the beauty of the countryside, the hills, the valleys, and clear blue streams. It was truly beautiful to behold.

We left Scotland and made our way to our next port-of-call, Gutenberg, Sweden. I believe our stay was three days and I thoroughly enjoyed every moment. I have never seen so many beautiful women in my life. My most memorable time, however, was at a dance. I had asked a taxi driver to take me to a place where there was dancing. He did all right; he took me to a ballroom dance. Not knowing it was ballroom dancing; I entered the building and witnessed one of the most beautiful spectacles that I have ever seen in my life or have ever seen since. Was this a dream? This just couldn't be happening. Was I on the set of a Walt Disney movie? As I looked around, I felt so out of place, and I was even wearing my dress blue's. I was in awe and totally captivated as I watched full flowing Cinderella evening gowns; Prince Charming tuxedos complete with tails, all swirling around on the dance floor, waltzing to the live music of a full-compliment orchestra who were also dressed in formal attire. It was Heaven on Earth.

We shipped out again. This time though, we were on a mission.

As we neared our destination, somewhere in the North Atlantic, planes flew overhead and began examining us very closely. Very closely! We, meaning the crew of the *'Valcour'* had no idea what these planes were doing, nor did we know who they were, but as bits of information began to trickle down the tubes from the top, we learned that they were Soviet surveillance planes. This information would be substantiated very shortly.

Within a day we picked up a visitor, a soviet, guided missile destroyer. Our visitor followed our every move for the next three weeks. At one point, when we had to refuel at sea, the destroyer nosed its bow between the *Valcour* and our supply ship. Possibly being curious as to our technique of 'high lining' fuel and supplies, the destroyer nosed close enough to our fantails that we were able to make rude gestures and yell obscenities. During one of the transfers of our much-needed provisions, a few of us watched in horror as a bundle came loose from the 'high line' and in an instant, disappeared into the frigid ocean. It was our precious mail and now it was gone! Gone forever. No 'Mail Call' that day and certainly, no homemade cookies that I could mooch from my friends. It brought back a memory of the first care package that I had I received. My sister had sent me some homemade goodies and I shared most of them with my friends. It wasn't because of my generosity; it was because I wanted to show my friends that I had a family that cared too. It made me very proud and happy.

No homemade goodies for anyone this time, that is, except for the fish. Oh well, at least we got to make rude gestures and yell obscenities to these 'commies.'

We still didn't have the big picture of what this operation was all about, but we knew that part of our duty was to drop small depth charges into the ocean at certain intervals. According to scuttlebutt, this would obstruct sonar signals of soviet submarines.

Our watch during this deployment was four hours on, and four hours off. The four hours off didn't count during regular working hours because we still had to carry out our regular duties. For example, four hours on watch at 4:00 am, four hours on duty at 8:00 am, four hours on watch at 12:00 pm and then starting at 4:00 pm, four hours of R&R and chow, only to be interrupted by a half hour to relieve the 4:00 pm watch for his chow. Surprising, as it may seem, the USN does not pay overtime.

After standing my 4:00 am to 8:00 am watch, I went topside for some fresh air but I got a lot more than fresh air. I was greeted by a view that was beyond belief. I was looking at the entire naval fleet of the Soviet Union, or so it had appeared. It was massive! Almost completely surrounded by this Soviet Armada was the *Valcour*, a large American task force of destroyers' and me. In the middle of all this, were two gigantic U.S. Navy cable layers, with their cable reels coming together at the bow. The end result of this mission would have been the splicing of the two ends of their cables together. This was extra shocking because all this time at sea we did not see a single ship other than our sniffing soviet destroyer. Suddenly, a startling announcement was made. "General Quarters!" "Man your battle stations!" I had a momentary thought that the 'cold war' was about to warm up, and that the waters of the North Atlantic wasn't warm.

Shortly after manning our stations, another announcement was made, this time it was made by the Commanding Officer, "Attention all hands. This is your Captain speaking. We have just received orders to take defensive action should soviet aggression jeopardize the success of our mission. Carry on." 'There was no bridge over these troubled waters' I thought.

I don't remember exactly how long it was before the next announcement but we heard, "All engines!" Full speed ahead." I thought, 'full speed ahead to where, the side of a soviet destroyer?' Strangely enough, the suddenness of it all, and the intrigue, far outweighed any fear that I might have had, other than the thought of the North Atlantic being mighty cold.

The next announcement, about an hour later, was less ominous and was welcomed news; General Quarters was cancelled and we operated at the second highest level of alert. I was relieved from my battle station, the electrical control room, by the normally scheduled watch and went topside. And once more I was witnessing another amazing site, the American Fleet in staggered formation, and as far as my eye could see, was being 'chased' by the Soviet Fleet. I thought, 'what the hell's going on?'

I guess the C.O. read my thoughts because he made an announcement that the *'Valour'* was to chart a course to Norfolk, Virginia, and depending upon the circumstances at the halfway point, our orders could be revised.

Shortly afterward, we were finally put in the big picture.

The original and overall objective of the United States Navy was to lay a cable from somewhere in Europe, France I believe it was, across the Atlantic to a naval base in Newfoundland, Canada. The cable, however, was being laid across a soviet 'playground' in the North Atlantic. The 'playground' is where soviet ships carry out naval tests and manoeuvres, similar to a U.S. naval 'playground' in the southeast Atlantic Ocean.

The purpose of the cable, as was explained to me, was to pickup signals from any vessel crossing its path. Every ship, because of the nature of its mechanical equipment, has a 'signature.' The signature could derive from the intrinsic design of a single pump, motor or shaft. This signature, through means of sophisticated intelligence gathering could identify exactly, the ship, county of origin, and more importantly, any abnormal or increased activity in the area.

The ultimate goal of our mission, in which the *Valcour* played a very minimal role, was to splice the cable. I don't know what took place during the last few minutes of the operation but with our fantails between our legs we headed home. Fishing trawlers, probably equipped with state of the art communication systems, soon replaced the soviet military fleet. We passed the halfway point, the point of no return, and still being followed, we returned to Norfolk Virginia.

CHAPTER 3

The USS Recovery

THE *'RECOVERY'* WAS a smaller ship than the *'Valcour'* but it didn't take long for me to adjust to my new surroundings. The *Recovery* also offered me a new and valuable experience in the electrical trade; the ship was completely Direct Current. It was really quite unique. Equipped with a tugboat in tow, we were soon underway and I was heading back to the North Atlantic.

The mission was quite simple; complete the installation of a cable that was running across the North Atlantic and terminated in Newfoundland, Canada. Could this possibly be 'the cable' that almost caused a world war? Things started to make sense. The deep-sea divers aboard the *Recovery* could easily perform underwater cable splicing or any other work required but still not being privy to specific details of our assignment I would have to wait and see.

Besides the fascination of it all, I felt extremely privileged to watch deep-sea divers in action, well, when they were above the surface anyway. I thought to myself, "How many people in this word get the opportunity to observe the complete procedure of dressing, preparing, lifting, and lowering these extremely specialized hardhat divers into the ocean depths, and then to hear them talking to you from hundreds of feet below just as though they were only a few feet away." It was truly absorbing.

I remember a diver friend of mine 'Jim' telling me about his initial training. He was lowered to the depths, equipped with a fire hose. Once on the bottom and with the fire hose directed around his feet, the nozzle was opened. The high-pressure water caused tons of sand and sediment to rise above him; the nozzle was then closed, and the tons of sand and sediment fell, completely enveloping him. He was buried. Jim was not cloister phobic and he passed his test.

Upon completing whatever undersea work the divers did, the *Recovery* headed for Reykjavik, Iceland. On our approach we had the opportunity to observe the birth of a volcano, and it was eerie. There in the near distance, we could see hot vapours of steam rising from the ocean. There was no physical volcanic cone projecting from the ocean, just plumes of steam. It appeared as though the ocean surface was on fire. How could this be?

The purpose of our visit to this Island of the mighty Viking was not just to observe the birth of a volcano, but it was the second step of our assignment. This is where the tugboat that we had been towing came into use. Our team of divers were to install tiles over this mysterious 'cable' just off the shore of Iceland. The tiles would protect the cable from the ravages of surf and tide. This undertaking, however, didn't require deep-sea diving or even scuba diving. The divers, clad only in wet suits and flippers, didn't even need heavy leaded belts because the weight of each tile was sufficient enough to take the divers to the bottom, place the tile over the cable, and flipper back to the tugboat for another tile. After a few days, the tiles were in place and the *'Discovery'* headed toward Newfoundland.

Our first port of call was St. John's, the capital of the province of Newfoundland, Some of my mates had never been to Canada before, and because of their total ignorance of the country, they gave me the gears, as though, this quaint little fishing village represented what all the cities in Canada probably looked like. I have always had a tendency to ignore complete ignorance, especially when there is absolutely no hope of reform, and ignore I did. I do know however, that during our stay, they completely fell in love with St. John's.

I can't remember what our purpose in St. John's was, or if it was even related directly to the 'cable' but I'm sure it was. We set sail again and followed the coastline of the provinces, Avalon Peninsula until we reached Argentia, Newfoundland.

The naval base in Argentia had a nightclub and it was, fantastic! There was entertainment and dancing every night, and always to a live band. It was open to the public and more importantly, to the lovely ladies of Argentia, which makes sense, because I can't even fathom the thought of a bunch of sailors dancing around the dance floor together, although, to certain minorities, this would be a fantasy. Every night, it was wall-to-wall happiness. I had never been entertained by the USO before, but the entertainment that they provided for us one night, was spectacular! They made us all feel good. There was no Bob Hope, but I can now truly relate to, and appreciate, all of the good feelings that Bob and his performers instilled on troupes while serving overseas, and how all of their anxieties could be completely erased, even if it was for one short evening.

One night, while I was sitting at the bar enjoying a finely brewed Canadian beer, I looked toward the dance floor, and there, dressed in red, was a beautiful young lady, dancing with two of her girl friends to a lively tune. She was so beautiful and she was so graceful, my heart started racing.

Erroneously, I had always thought of myself, as 'God's Gift to Women' and I also thought, that 'women should view me as a special gift.' Yuk! Barf! In reality however, I was shy, insecure and totally inept when it came to speaking with the opposite sex.

With shaking knees however, I approached the Lady in Red and asked her to dance. She accepted, and other than taking the occasional break, we danced all night. She was so graceful, and I don't know how, and I don't know why, but I made moves on that dance floor like I have never made before or have ever made since. We were perfect dance partners. We just clicked.

Strangely enough, not once did I sit with her and her friends, nor did I offer to buy her a drink. I'm not really sure why, but it was probably a combination of shyness and nervousness. Our only conversations took place during slow dances, and as was the norm at the time, the final dance was slow. I asked her if she was coming back the next night, she smiled and replied that she hadn't planned on it, but "Yes I'll be here."

The next night after some skilful planning, I was ready to dance! I forget how I did it, but I snuck off the ship dressed in my 'Mohammad' tailored, blue sports jacket, black slacks, and I was looking good! The Lady in Red was there, but she was not wearing red, she was wearing blue! I believe that we were both equally happy to see each other, but she looked a little surprised to see me in civvies. Looking back, I don't think it was the wearing of civvies that shocked her, but it was the civvies I was wearing. Oh well! We clicked again. This night however, we drew a crowd. We were so into our moves that we didn't realize at first that we were the only two on the dance floor. It seemed that everyone in the club had moved to the outside perimeter of the dance floor and were clapping us on. Wow! John Travolta and Olivia Newton John before their time. This happened more than once that night, and again the next night, and it will be forever etched in my memory. It was, and it still is, hard for me to believe, that after three evenings of one-on-one dancing, laughing and enjoying each other's company, we never once sat alone together, nor did we ever kiss.

Having accomplished our 'cable' mission successfully, and before leaving Argentia, and of course my 'Lady in Red,' the Commanding Officer requested permission from H.Q. to make a little detour on our return home to Norfolk, VA. Permission granted! "Anchors a Way My Boys, Anchors Away!" Down the St. Lawrence River we sailed, and on to Montreal,

Quebec to attend the World Exposition 'Expo 67.' So much for that, let's go home now. Are we there yet? Personally I found both 'Expo 67' and Montreal to be a complete disappointment. The only thing that Montreal did for me was prove to some of my ignorant shipmates that all Canadian cities weren't all clapboard sided fishing village buildings, but then again and after some consideration, I would hope that their fondest memory of Canada was St. Johns and Argentia Newfoundland, and I'm sure it was.

Norfolk, V.A. here I come, and this is where I would spend my last few weeks in the United States Navy.

Farewell 'Recovery'

A FEW DAYS after our return to Norfolk, I was informed that the Commanding Officer wanted to see me in his quarters. Gee, what an honour. I had never been in a captain's quarters before and I knew for sure that it wasn't for disciplinary reasons, because I hadn't been in trouble for months. "Summers reporting as requested Sir." The C.O. cordially invited me to sit down. "So, Summers, I understand that your enlistment is up soon." "Yes Sir." I replied. "Well, have you given any thought to shipping over?" "No Sir, I don't think the navy is the life for me." "Well," he said smiling, "That's what I had thought at one time, but after giving it a lot of serious consideration, I decided to make it, the life for me. And now as I look back, I made the right choice." "Yes Sir." I respectfully replied. He continued on to say that the navy has a lot to offer besides the travel, variety, and adventure. What I really wanted to say was; been there, done that, but this phrase wasn't in use at the time so I just remained silent. Still smiling he said, "Summers, do you realize, that if you extend your enlistment for another six years you will receive a six thousand dollar shipping-over bonus, and for the first two years, you can be stationed anywhere in the world that you want?" An offer like that was certainly tempting, but I also knew that I had up to three months after my discharge to make up my mind. I also knew that it would be a feather in his cap if I were to ship over on his watch. I respectfully declined the offer. "Very well Summers" he replied, "You are dismissed."

The very next day a surprise inspection was called. While the C.O. walked through the ranks, he stopped at me, inspected my uniform and said, "Summers, your dress blues look a little tattered." "They do Sir?" I replied in surprise. "Yes they do. They are a disgrace. I order you to purchase a new uniform by the end of this week." I was stunned. I was irate, but I managed to contain myself and replied in a quiet but disappointed voice, "Yes Sir." But I thought, "You bastard!" I had less than two weeks before my discharge, and because I upset this asshole by not shipping over, I had to buy a new uniform. I had other 'Lovable' thoughts as well.

But a remarkable thing happened the next day that even the C.O. probably didn't expect. I was immediately transferred to shore duty on the naval base for the processing of my discharge papers. Hey captain! Shove your order for me to purchase a new uniform up your fantail.

The USS Recovery

Reflections

FOR A COUPLE of days while my mustering out papers was being processed, I was assigned to shore patrol. I would simply stroll the streets of the base and be on the lookout for I really don't know what. Although this was a monotonous assignment, it gave me plenty of time to think. And think I did.

I reflected back on all the events that lead up to my being here. After my mother had passed away, I went to live with my Uncle Earl and Aunt Edith. They owned a farm and didn't have children. Without my knowledge my father had made this arrangement with them after my mother's funeral. Working on the farm was a wonderful experience and I enjoyed it immensely. I worked very hard to prove my worth and the harder I worked the more I enjoyed it. Earl tried very hard to urge me into going back to school but I wasn't ready for a one-room schoolhouse, education. There had to be a better way. Then one day he announced that he landed me a job at the Camp Ipperwash army base just a few miles away. Earl was a well-respected man in the community and he had a lot of influence. He must have had, to be able to get me a plum civil service job without my going through an interview. My interests had always been electrically oriented, and I was given an electrical apprenticeship in the engineering section at the base. I had recently purchased a 1956 Ford Meteor with the five hundred dollars that my mother had left me which allowed me travel to and from work without relying on Earl for a ride. I would rise each morning at five o'clock, carry out my farm chores, and work eight hours at the base and then return at night to do chores again. It was summertime so after dinner there was fieldwork as well. I didn't mind in anyway, in fact I thrived on it. Although I enjoyed both jobs, there was still something missing.

My supervisor, at the army base was a wonderful person. His name was Wes and he was so easy to work for. He was also very easy to talk to. During one of our conversations, I had mentioned to him that my lack of a High School education bothered me somewhat, but at the same time I was turned off the idea of a one-room schoolhouse setting. He then suggested that there was another way that I could possibly get my diploma. He asked, "Have you ever thought about joining the armed forces?" The seed was planted.

Farewell Earl, Edith and Wes

IT WASN'T LONG after the seed was planted that I packed my bags, bid farewell to my wonderful aunt and uncle and headed home to Windsor. I was going to join the navy. As a youngster, I had been in the Army, Air and Sea Cadets and it was the Sea Cadets that I enjoyed the most.

I moved in with my dad's lady friend Elvira while I was preparing to join the navy. She didn't mind because she liked me, and I think she liked me more than my naivety would allow me think. She had a daughter living at home and another daughter married and living a short distance away. They liked me as well, even more than my naivety would allow me to think.

The next morning I headed to the Canadian Naval Recruitment Office where I was required to take an entrance exam and fill out an application form. After successfully completing both, I was brought in to talk to the recruiter. I don't know if this guy was having a bad day or having a bad life because his first question was, "Are you enjoying life at present?" To which I simply replied, "Yes."

He then said a most shocking thing! "Well, stay out of the navy then!" At first I thought he was joking. But this was no a joke, he was serious. Here was a naval recruiter that within one instant of time prevented the Canadian Navy from recruiting a young, eager, and qualified candidate. I definitely stayed out of that navy.

Later while telling my friends about this strange happening, one of them said, "Why don't you look into the US Navy? They accept Canadians." Another seed was planted and across the Windsor, Detroit boarder I went. Talk about a whole different story! I entered the recruitment office and was warmly greeted by a very happy looking Chief Petty Officer. He was very stout and was enjoying a huge cigar that projected from his mouth. He shook my hand and asked what he could do for me. I told him that I was a Canadian citizen, and I was interested in what the US Navy had to offer me. Cigar out of his mouth and with a gruff, but likable voice he said "Anything you want! Just sign here on the dotted line." "But what about education, what type of education can I get?" I asked. "We'll send you to Harvard, just sign here my boy." I continued on, "How about advancement opportunities?" "You my friend, will be an admiral before you know it, just sign here." I signed my name, filled out an application form, took an entrance exam and after waiting a couple of months for my visa, I was soon on my way to Boot Camp in sunny San Diego, California.

November 14, 1963

ON THE DAY of my departure, my father and sister accompanied me to the recruiting centre. Before leaving however, my dad suggested that I change from the checker pants I was wearing to something more suitable. "No way dad! This is the latest style." Off to Detroit we went, and after a few hugs, some words of encouragement and of course a few tears. I was on my own. I entered the recruitment centre with mixed emotions.

There were about twenty of us new recruits, and we were asked to raise our right hand and take an oath. The oath was our official inauguration into the United States Navy. Standing at the back of the group, I repeated the oath as instructed but I didn't raise my right hand. This was just in case I didn't like being in the navy I could simply go home.

After arriving in San Diego, a military bus transported us to the naval base. When the gates closed behind us I started to get the feeling that I might have made a mistake. That feeling got stronger over the next few hours while we were being processed. I really didn't like the attitude of these people that were yelling and swearing at us. No one has ever talked like that to me before.

We probably hit our bunks about 2 a.m. and it felt like I just got to sleep when someone using a huge steel garbage can with a metal hammer, banged us into instant consciousness. I thought: Hey! That's rude, at the swearing in, I didn't raise my right hand, so I want to go home. So much for that loophole!

I have two fond memories as I look back at those three months in boot. The first was on Christmas Eve. Our 'Company' was on mess duty. It was a horrible two-week assignment and we slaved for twelve hours a day. I was scrubbing metal food trays, hundreds of them, when orders came that I was to return to the company barracks immediately because I was promoted to Training Petty Officer. As I ran across the massive parade square towards the barracks, I heard a choir singing in the distance, and for the first time in my life, I felt the true spirit of Christmas. When I reached the barracks, I was congratulated by my fellow petty officers and given my first training assignment. I was to train, and prepare, my 'Company' for a mock disaster aboard the USS Recruit. The ship was a replica of a navy ship, mounted on cement, which was used for various training exercises. This introduction to 'training' would later become one of the most important skills that I would possess in life.

While being briefed on my training assignment, I was also told that if even a single recruit fails this exercise, I would be put back two weeks in boot camp. The word 'motivation' comes to mind. I was motivated.

Of course during my 'lectures' I would get the odd threat by someone that they were going to deliberately fail, but it didn't come to that because I experienced my first success.

My second fondest memory took place on the final day of boot camp. A group of us were reminiscing about how we had all changed over the past three months when one person asked, "Do you guys remember that idiot that got off the bus wearing chequered pants?" After a little laughter, I piped in and said. "Yea what a jerk, who was he anyway?" No one knew except me.

Simply put, Boot Camp was pure hell but I endured. It would take a while for me to realise it, but that training and discipline, was the best thing that could have ever happened to me.

After boot camp we were allowed a two-week leave before reporting to our next assignment. I returned to Windsor. After a three-month absence, my family and friends were absolutely astonished by the change in my appearance and the change in me. My sister pointed out the most notable change. It was my tan and the thickness of my hair. I must admit that my hair did grow back very nicely after being shaved bald on my second day in boot, but I hadn't realized at the time that I had acquired such a nice tan. I think my three-months in San Diego during the depths of winter had something to do with it. I had a wonderful, although fast two-week leave, and soon it was time to fly back to California and begin my training at the San Diego Naval Training Centre.

During boot, I took a series of exams in order to qualify for entry to the 'Electrician Mate Training School.' I qualified, and on my first day of school, the instructor motivated me, and the entire class to succeed, by saying, "This training program requires that you to take an exam at the end of every week. Should you fail, even one weekly exam, you will be expelled, you will be transferred out, and you will probably spend the rest of your naval career, chipping and painting the side of a ship." I was motivated, and I excelled. After three months I graduated, and stitched another stripe on my uniform.

CHAPTER 4

Farewell 'U.S. Navy'

HAVING RECEIVED MY transfer papers, my personnel file documents, mustering out pay, and my airline ticket, I was now a civilian. I didn't really look like one because I had to wear my 'tattered' dress blues in order to fly at the reduced rate offered to the military. I had one final thought. "Maybe I should have obeyed the captain's orders and purchased a new uniform for this special occasion." Yea right!

I'd be lying if I said that this was one of the happiest moments of my life because; although there is an experience of euphoria and a rush of adrenaline at a time like this, there is also the fear of the unknown. The truth is, the navy looked after me for four years, and looked after me very well. I was clothed, fed, educated, entertained and paid to travel to exotic places that most people can only read about. But now comes the unknown. What the heck, look out Canada and civilian life, here I come!

My flight home had a stopover in Chicago at the O'Hare airport. It was a fairly lengthy stop over so I just roamed about, sat about and basically watched my soon to be peers, 'civilians.' There was one group of civilians that caught my interest in particular. 'Businessmen.' I was impressed by the way they dressed, wearing expensive looking suits, polished shoes (these stood out to me in particular) and brief cases that probably contained important documents. My mind reflected back to my father who had been a successful businessman and managed a well-known paper company. I remembered back to when he would fly away on business and my mother would take us to the airport to see him off. When his plane took off I would think, "Wow he must be an important person."

I, myself, didn't really know what I was going to do when I got home, other than find some kind of job while I decided, but one of my good mates, no! One of my good friends had once commented that he thought I would make a good sales man. Hey! Maybe it's in my blood? But first I have to learn to speak civilian.

My fight landed in Detroit. I crossed the border to Windsor and of course, the very first thing I did was go see my 'daddy!' Well? I needed some place to live.

The Royal Tavern

MY DAD HAD a sizable apartment above the Royal Tavern. It offered a panoramic view of a very busy and very noisy main street with neon lights flashing from the movie theatre across the street, bright florescent lights from a large grocery store and an array of small retail stores. My dad allowed me to stay with him until I could find my own accommodations. These living quarters were far and away from what my father had been accustomed to at one time in his life. It was a little unsettling to think that such a successful businessman could resort to living like this, above a tavern of all things, but it was his choice, and he was very content. Shortly after I left for the navy, he packed in his position as a company manager, took a job at a local marina and worked as a labourer. His reason? There was no longer the desire, or the need to continue on in a competitive and stressful business environment. He enjoyed his job and the physical labour. He was happy. C'est la vie!

My dad had a new girl friend and she lived in the apartment next door. Her nickname was Mil. They were good company for each other, and because she had her own apartment, I didn't feel that I would be a hindrance in their relationship. I knew that my stay would be short term anyway.

Adjusting to civilian life was a little difficult at times, and one major adjustment was trying to sleep in a civilian bed. My bed was small, but being small was not the problem, I was use to that. It was the mattress. It was soft and thick and was supported by yet another thick-coiled mattress. This, compared to the one-inch thick mattress supported by a tightly stretched canvas that I had slept on for four years, presented a problem. For a few weeks, I slept on the floor and then gradually adjusted to a civilian bed. Staying at the Royal Tavern, however, did help in some ways to adjust to this different way of life. We didn't cook in the apartment, so for lunch and dinner, we would simply go down below, and chow down in the galley. Sorry about that, what I meant to say was, we would simply go down stairs and dine in the restaurant. I will get it right; I'm still adjusting. For breakfast, we would walk to the corner greasy spoon and dine on grease.

Our rent also included maid service, which was a step up from the navy. Our racks, I mean our beds would be made, and the sheets would be changed at regular intervals. The maid did say, however, that she had never changed floor sheets before. In the end, the Royal Tavern did turn out to be a good place for me to adapt to civilian life.

On the day I was discharged, I had received a sum of money that was owed to me for whatever reason, and as well; I had been buying U.S. Savings Bonds through payroll deductions for the past two years. This money afforded me a little financial support during my civilian reincarnation, but it was running out and it was time to find a job.

I had 'Salesman" in mind, so I decided to apply for a sales position at the J. L. Hudson Department Store in Detroit. The reason behind this decision was my mother. She had worked for a number of years at 'Hudson's' and worked her way up the ladder from a sales clerk to a management position. I thought that her previous status and her work performance at Hudson's might help me to secure a position. It did. I got a job as a sales clerk in the hardware department. Being a sales clerk required the wearing of a suit and tie, so I immediately purchased a rather expensive suit of clothes, and a very expensive pair of shoes. I forget the name of them but they had these little tiny indents on the toe of the shoe. I saw a lot of important looking businessmen at the O'Hare airport wearing them. So, "When in Rome..." It turned out however, that they weren't really good for spit polishing. I also purchased a Fedora. That was a bit of a mistake and a little passé' but I was now ready to become a successful businessman.

I took a bus across the border each day to my new place of employment, determined to sell enough hardware to exceed my quotas. This would be no problem I thought because Christmas was fast approaching and everyone would want to buy someone some hardware. I must admit however, that there is a little more to selling hardware than I had thought. I learned that it takes much more than just being courteous and presentable, you actually have to know your product. Who would guess? I never did exceed my quota; in fact I never once, reached my quota. Christmas came and went, and as per usual in the retail business, everyone in the world had enough hardware to last them until the next Christmas. But wait! Women never have enough shoes to last them for even a week, so I transferred to the Women's Shoe Department. Even though I haven't seen many women's shoes in the past four years, it made perfect sense to me that I should sell 'women's' shoes. My reason? I could sell a pair of shoes to a woman and at the same time, give her lessons on how to spit shine them. I knew absolutely zilch about shoes, men's or women's, but I was given the job to sell them and sell them I would. No problem! I loved women and because of that, I would exceed my quota.

It was a great job but there was one drawback. It was the new era of the mini skirt and high length boots that were 'made for walking.'

Just imagine for a moment my predicament though, I am on my knees, a beautiful young lady is seated in front of me, I am facing, at eye level, a pair of legs that go all the way to the top, and the view of the top was only interrupted by one foot of skirt material. As I struggled to fit a pair of high length boots on these magnificent legs, it required each leg to be lifted so that I could pull the boot almost to that top. The drawback to the job, however, was the words, "I'll take them." I was completely unable to stand up for quite some time; therefore, I never met my quota in that department either.

During this time of enduring the 'hard'-ships of working in the shoe department, my dad had introduced me to a friend of his while we were enjoying a beer at the bar. He worked as an operator at a coal fired generating station. The next weekend he took me on a tour and as I walked through the station I thought to myself,

"This is the place for me." Although the power plant was a hundred times bigger than that of a naval ship, the basic principles were the same. I asked him how I would go about getting a job as an electrician at the station; he simply gave me the name of the electrical foreman. From there I was on my own and the rest was up to me. The next week I took a day off from the shoe department, to rest my 'knees' and with some papers in hand I headed to the power station. I went to the guardhouse and told security that I wanted to see Mr. Jack Lay. He asked me if I had an appointment, to which I replied that I didn't and that I only wanted a few minutes of Jack Lay's time. Security called through and Jack gave the okay for me to enter the station. As instructed, I took the elevator, walked down a hallway, past the administration offices and entered the electrical shop. I asked for Mr. Jack Lay and was shown his office. His door was open, so I entered and introduced myself. We shook hands, and I assertively told him that I would like a job as an electrician. He was a bit taken back at the suddenness of all of this and asked me how I got his name. I gave the name of the person, and explained that he had given me a tour of the plant. Jack then explained to me that there was a formal process in the company, as is the case in most companies, when applying for employment. He continued to say that it was most unusual for a stranger to just burst in and say that he wanted a job. Getting that off his chest he asked what my credentials were.

I explained my background and experience, and handed him some of my certificates including my performance ratings from the navy. He was quite impressed by the comments that were made on my performance rating sheets, as I was when I first read them myself. There was no mention of my being 'Loveable.' Just that I was a good electrician, I was reliable, dependable, a good senior petty officer while I was in charge of the ships electrical shop, and that I was an asset to the U.S. Navy. He then said, "It just so happens that I will need a good electrician soon. One of my crew will be retiring." With that he handed me an application form and told me to leave it at the guardhouse when it was completed. The next day, my 'knees' still weren't relaxed enough so I took another day off. I filled out the application and delivered it as instructed. Two weeks later I got a letter from the generating station asking me to attend an interview the following week. Gee, another day off? My 'knees' were going to turn into mush.

The day came for my interview and I was not the least bit nervous, probably because I was a little hung over from celebrating my impending interview the night before. I have always been a little 'cart before the horse.'

I showed up for my interview dressed in the uniform of a typical electrician, a suit and tie, with spit shined shoes. I was taken by a secretary to the boardroom where I was introduced by Jack Lay to the Station Maintenance Superintendent, the Personnel Officer, and an Engineer. I was then asked to be seated. After a few niceties the interview began. Most of the questions where of course, technical in nature but some were goal oriented. I was ready for both. The superintendent 'hinted' to me that I was lacking experience in the power generation industry, and that if I were to be selected for the position, I could possibly be offered a job at a lesser rate that would require a further two years of on the job training before being certified as a station electrician. I don't know if it was my hang over or whether it was my arrogance, but boy was I was cocky. With my arm draped over the backrest of the chair, my suit jacket unbuttoned, I responded by saying that I felt that I was qualified enough for the job, and that the need for additional training was not required. Generating station experience would come naturally and quickly, and that it would not be a hindrance to my performance. What the heck I thought, "If worse comes to worse I already had a job that would keep me in good shape and turn my mushy knees, hard." That was basically the end of the interview; I was thanked for attending and told that they would let me know.

It was about two weeks later that I received a letter from Ontario Hydro. The letter was brief and to the point, it offered me the position of Shift Electrician at the J. Clark Keith Generating Station. It stated my salary, union requirements, and shift differential benefits. It was signed by the Station Manager, Mr. Stewart McPhail. I did it! I did it! Oh, sorry! Thanks again mom. I was ecstatic, but I don't think there was anybody happier than my father. Besides the idea of me getting a good job in one of the best industries in all of Canada, he would finally get his apartment back all to himself, and I would also be able to afford to buy that dinner for four, finally paying off that year old gambling debt when my dad hustled me at the pool table.

It was kind of ironic though; my commencement date with Ontario Hydro was February the 14, 1968. The final date for my shipping over in the USN in order to reap the $6000 benefit for doing so was also February the 14th 1968. Well, been there, done that. It was time for change, but first; it was time for a celebration. "Hey dad, do you want to buy us some beers, I'll pay you back?"

CHAPTER 5

Ontario Hydro

The J. Clark Keith Generating Station

THE MORNING CAME for me to report to my new job, and although I would miss all of those lovely legs, this job was more suited to my vocation. I left the Royal early, dined on some grease, and arrived at the station about an hour and a half early. After waking the security guard, he phoned the electrical shop to get my clearance. Once granted, I headed for the station thinking, "Gee I hope I didn't wake the midnight shift as well." The electrician on shift was a bit surprised by all this because no one had told him that I was coming, especially at this time of the morning.

He did hear, however, that someone had been hired, but he didn't know any of the details.

I have always felt that when I meet people for the first time, I was very good at reading their vibes, and I was now reading some negative vibes. I would soon find out why. After some discussion about what the job entails, a few other electricians began to filter in, and finally Jack Lay. Jack introduced me to everyone, starting with the sub-Forman. We then sat down in his office for a brief orientation before taking me to the stores where I was issued my personal protective equipment. From there he took me on a tour of the station introducing me to a few hundred people along the way.

I liked Jack from the first moment I met him, and as time would tell, that 'like' would grow into a paramount respect.

After completing our tour, Jack took me to the Maintenance Superintendent's office where Mr. Keith Wigget warmly greeted me. After welcoming me aboard, and offering me a few words of encouragement, we got up to leave and I said, "Thank you Mr. Wigget" to which he responded, "Please, call me Keith." As I left his office I thought that it would be quite impossible for me to call him by his first name. It wasn't just because of my navy discipline, but because I was raised to respect my elders and to address them as Mr, Mrs, or Sir, especially people in prominent positions. From 'Keith's' office we dropped in on 'Stew,' I mean Mr. Stewart McPhail, the Station Manager. Once again, after a few niceties, we stood up to leave, and I said, "Thank you, Mr. McPhail," to which he simply replied, "You're welcome."

My first day basically consisted of meeting people, and before the day was over I was given a list of tools that I was required to purchase within a week. I immediately thought, "Dad I need more money!"

There was one other thing that Jack brought to my attention before I left work. It was my clothes. When I reported for work that morning I had been dressed in a pair of casual slacks, and a pair of fairly shiny casual shoes. I knew I had been receiving some negative vibes but hey! Clothes don't make the electrician. I really didn't have any work clothes, although I guess I should have thought about that before reporting to work in an industrial coal fired generating station. Well I certainly would have work clothes by the next morning. "Dad, I need more and more money!"

Not far from the Royal Tavern there was a clothing store that sold work clothes, and they were open until 6 pm. With my father's money in hand, I purchased two sets of pants and shirts, and a pair of work shoes. The tool purchase could wait until the weekend. The next morning I was ready for work looking every bit like a professional electrician. Arriving early as per my usual, I was greeted by the same electrician as the previous morning. His name was Ray. Once again, I got the same 'vibes' but I can now understand why. I looked like a TV commercial, advertising work clothes. I wore a neatly pressed pair of green pants with a matching, neatly pressed green shirt. My new work shoes weren't spit polished but to Ray they probably appeared that way.

Thank goodness the shift rotations were on a weekly basis so that Ray didn't see me when I showed up the following Monday morning. Over the weekend I had purchased most of the required tools from what would now be considered a discount store. They weren't the brand name tools that professionals would use, but my tool list didn't specify quality and besides, there was only so much money that my father could afford. My new tool pouch looked good though. It had a bright whitish tan with a soft suede texture. It sure looked good, and especially with my brand-new shiny red and blue tools protruding from it as it hung from the belt of my neatly pressed green uniform. When I boarded the morning bus, I felt proud. All of the people on the bus just stared at me as though they had never seen a professional electrician before. When my foreman arrived at work that morning he inspected my tools and just shook his head and said, "I'm sorry Gary, these will never do." 'Daddy dear, I need lots and lots and lots more money.' I look back now and just shudder to think about those discount tools that I had bought.

Independence

I FINALLY FOUND my own apartment and my dad was pleased with the news, that is, until he found out its location. It was at the Royal Tavern, just down the hall from him.

My next priority was getting a drivers licence and finding some wheels. My brother-in-law Hal, offered to help me out. After getting my beginners licence, Hal gave me some refresher driver training. The last time that I drove a vehicle was in Philadelphia. My ship was in dry dock for a refit, and our Commanding Officer had been assigned a military jeep for his personal use. It was Christmas Eve, and the jeep was parked on the dock being of no good use to anyone. I approached the 'Officer of The Day' and asked permission to use the jeep to go to midnight mass. "Permission denied," he said. When I left the ship heading to find a church, any church, I passed by the jeep and noticed that the keys were left in the ignition. I pretentiously thought: "How can one individual deny me of my religious freedom?" So I borrowed the jeep and went to church. I prayed once more upon my return, "Thanks for me not getting caught." I do at times; move in mysterious ways, and I have often wondered why. Unlike the many questions I have had during my life, with their answers yet to come, including the big one, this answer is easy. 'God moves in mysterious ways and I merely follow him.

Hal picked me up one night outside the Royal Tavern in his candy apple red, speckled, Austin Healy convertible. It was beautiful, and it was his baby, besides his real baby Kristen, and of course his wife Bev. Our mission was to find me some wheels. I was looking for a convertible, I thought that with having one, all of the pretty young ladies in Windsor would want to ride with me, and they would stand in line waiting for their opportunity. I found a beauty on a used car lot. It was totally loaded, and the sales man told me that a doctor had previously owned it. I was tempted to buy it right then and there, but Hal in his wisdom cautioned me. He said, "Being previously owned by a doctor doesn't mean that it is a good used car. Doctors have a lot of money so they probably don't pay any attention to the maintenance upkeep because if the car craps out, they simply buy a new one." On we went. After checking out a few car lots we stopped at a Pontiac dealership. There, in the show room was a brand-new 1968, Pontiac Parisian convertible. "That's all she wrote." I put in an offer to buy it on condition of my obtaining a down payment. Here I am looking to buy a brand-new car and I didn't even have a down payment.

The next day after work, my dad accompanied me to a lending institution to co-sign my down payment loan. However, while at work that day, I started to have second thoughts. My first thought was, I was still on a three-month probationary period with no guarantee of permanent employment. My second thought was of the financial burden. I did experience some relief about my probationary period from my sub-Forman. When I explained my position to him and my concerns, he simply smiled and said, I don't think you have to worry very much about that. I also thought that I could just buy a used clunker for now. After all, all I really needed was transportation, and I could settle for giving a ride to the occasional lady who was hitchhiking and was in desperate need. I carried this last thought with me to the lending institution. When the time came for me to sign on the bottom line, I told my dad that I was backing out. He took me aside and encouraged me to take the loan and buy the car by saying, something like, "You have a good job, your single, and you can afford it. I signed my name, but a few months later I would come to regret it, for more reasons than one.

Regrets, I've had a few...

WHILE I WAS serving in the navy I had corresponded with a young lady that I knew from childhood, and when I was on leave I would take her to out to a dance or something. When I got out of the navy, she was my first date, and I took her to the hottest disco in town. I was dressed to the hilt. I wore my red 'Mohammed' blazer, black pants and I even bought a new dress shirt. It was a shirt that would normally be worn with a tux. My tie was the bee's knees, it wasn't quite a bow tie, but it was similar to a bow that you would find on a Christmas present, and it was also red. I wore my beautiful white trench coat as well. Before I left to pick her up, I went down to the bar for a quick one, false courage so to say. While at the bar, a patron that I was not familiar with asked me if I played in some sort of band or something. It certainly makes sense to me now. Here I was in the era of 'Beatle' haircuts, miniskirts and denims. Oh well, to the dance we went, and I do remember that I had her in stitches with some of my stories, not navy stories however, because someone once advised me not to yak on and on about the navy, because people would just become bored, and tune me out.

At the end of the night we went to the coat check only to find out that my trench coat was stolen. I loved that trench coat and I was furious. I took my date home in a cab. The next day my dad took me back to the disco, and no matter what we said, or threatened to do to that establishment, it was all in vain. My trench coat was gone forever, and I have never seen a coat like it since. I would rather it had been my red blazer and shirt stolen. I probable wouldn't even have complained. Over the next few weeks we dated.

She was pretty and a very nice person, but I think her feelings toward me were much stronger than mine towards her. I just knew she wasn't the one for me. It all came to a head one Saturday night when I was at the bar of the Royal Tavern. I had earlier in the day told her that I wasn't interested in going out that evening, and then, as I was standing at the bar I heard her voice behind me, saying, "If you think I'm going to sit at home all alone on a Saturday night you've got another thing coming." That was it. Game over.

I felt really bad, and I sincerely regret the whole situation, and still do, because I really didn't think at the time, that there was the possibility of me leading her on to think that we were more romantically involved than we actually were.

CHAPTER 6

Barbara

I DIDN'T SPEND every Saturday night at the bar of the Royal Tavern; however, I was standing at the bar one Saturday night when my attention was drawn towards a table that was located near the dance floor. There were four people seated at the table. Three were middle aged, but I was only focusing on the fourth. With just one look, my heart was thumping. She was so beautiful! She had dark hair, and was wearing a pinkish dress with matching lipstick. She was just sitting, smiling and talking. Although I possessed a natural hindrance of being shy when first meeting a lady, I knew that I had to do something in order to get her attention, and without going through a clumsy and awkward introduction. I asked Ken, the bartender, for a clean, white bar towel. With the bar towel draped over my left arm I approached her table. I introduced myself as their new waiter and asked if they would like to order a drink. A pleasant "No Ta" was the reply. I then smiled and confessed that I wasn't a waiter; it was just that I wanted to introduce myself; and at that point, I offered to buy them a drink. I don't remember if they accepted my offer or not but the ice was broken. I returned to the bar so that I could regain my self-composure. When the time was right and I had stopped shaking, I approached the table again. I was asked to sit down and was introduced to everyone. One was Harry, a piano player and the evening's entertainment. The other was his wife Frieda, and I don't remember who the third one was because my main interest was the lady in pink. Harry and Frieda had lived in Oldham, Lancashire, England and were friends of Barbara's parents. They had three young children and Barbara baby sat for them from time to time. Frieda and Harry had been in the stages of immigrating to Canada when Barbara, for her own reasons, asked if she could join them. She would pay her own way, and help out with minding their children. Once in Canada, she would get a job and not be a burden. The deal was struck, and now here I was with Barbara sitting next to me. Towards the end of the evening I worked up the courage and asked her for a date. She accepted and we agreed that it would be the following Saturday night.

Work the following week was pure hell, not only for me, but also for my foreman, Jack Lay. I was in another world, and I really didn't know that it was that apparent until Jack called me in to his office. He pointed out a few of my blunders during the week and asked where my head was. I told him about the lady in pink, and that I couldn't stop thinking about her. With that he responded, "Well you better start thinking about your work or else!"

At last, Saturday night finally came and I took Barbara on our first date. I didn't want to take her to a tavern or a disco but somewhere more romantic, somewhere cosy and quiet. I remembered a bistro in Detroit where I occasionally had lunch after enduring a 'hard' morning on my knees selling shoes to mini skirters. It was late spring and I happily picked up Barbara in my convertible with the top down. Having only eaten lunch at this bistro, I didn't realize that in the evening it transformed into a wonderful and romantic dinner club. With the piano playing soft music and Barbara on my arm, we were seated at a candle lit table just on the edge of heaven. I didn't do a lot of talking that evening for the simple reason that I was totally love-struck. I can't pin point exactly why, other than it was just everything. Over the candlelight we basically gazed into each other's eyes, held hands and with soft music in the background I blurted out, "Will you marry me." I don't know who was more surprised at these words, her or me but I think she was, because she didn't answer me. In fact, that was basically the end to a wonderful evening. We quietly walked to my car, and as I opened the door for her, I noticed something missing. I had left the convertible top down and because of that, something very important to me was stolen, my seat cushion. The Pontiac was a big car and I being a mere 5 feet, six-and- a-half inches, needed a seat cushion to comfortably see over the dashboard. So I uncomfortably drove her home while straining to look over the dash and thinking that Barbara might have suddenly become aware that I was not as tall as she had previously thought. And for a moment, I also imagined her picturing me as needing wooden blocks on the gas and brake pedals.

I saw Barbara the next day. We didn't do anything special; we just sat around her house and talked. I also got to know a little bit about Harry, Frieda and their children especially one little six-year-old terror named Roger. He would simply go up to someone and kick him or her for no reason. Putting that aside and my bruises, I really enjoyed being there. It had been a long time since I experienced being with a family, and it felt good. I wouldn't be able to see Barbara (nee Cushnahan) for a week because I had to work the mid-night shift, and Barb, as I now called her, was enrolled in an adult education program during the day, studying to get her Canadian High School Diploma. This meant that my sleeping time was in the evening during her home time. I did see Harry though, because we were both able to play golf during the day. We didn't really play golf we tried to play golf. I wasn't very good, but Harry! I don't think he ever propelled the golf ball higher than one inch off the ground.

I thought about Barb a lot during that week and some of the stories that she had told me about, like her life in England, and her adventures when coming to Canada. Harry had already been in Canada for about three months before bringing his family over and of course my Barb. He had bought a house on Central Ave in Windsor and he had also bought a car. In the evenings he played a piano at the Royal Tavern and on occasion, played at a piano bar downtown. Prior to coming to Canada, he owned a pub in England and playing a piano was a big part of his life. Before I met Barb I had occasionally seen Harry at the Royal and heard him play, but I had never really talked to him. Anyway, after bidding farewell to her mother, father, sister, brother and niece, Barb and Harry's family sailed out of Liverpool England on the Canard Lines, and after being screened by customs in Quebec City, they continued on to Montreal where they disembarked as landed immigrants. That was April 18, 1967. Harry was there to meet them and drove them to Windsor. The most incredible part of this story to me was the fact that the very first thing Harry did on their very first day in Windsor, was to drive Frieda and Barb to a Manpower Centre to apply for a job. He didn't mess around.

Another incredible thing to me about this story was the generosity of the Canadian Government. They not only recommended that Barb attend school to obtain her high school diploma, but they paid her to attend. Wow!

One day shortly after they arrived, Frieda and Barb set off in Harry's car to go someplace, and shortly after starting out Frieda screamed to Barb, "Look at that bloody idiot coming at us on the wrong side of the road." Frieda learned her first Canadian driving lesson very quickly when she realized that she was the bloody idiot. Another time shortly after, they were waiting for a bus to go downtown, when a bus did stop and asked them where they were going, they found out once again that they were on the wrong side of the road and could have ended up far away in the opposite direction. Bloody hell!

In and out of shift work I would see Barb every chance I could get. One day, at the

Power plant, I was doing some work on the roof of an emergency gas generator. I forget the exact nature of the work, but it was a really hot day, and I was thinking how nice it would be to be at the beach. Bingo! After work I picked up Barb and off to the beach we went. We didn't have swimsuits so we went swimming in our skivvies. After drying off we took turns in the car to remove our wet skivvies and put on our dry clothes. We walked around for a bit and because Barb didn't have a bra on I got increasingly horny. These were the days before women went braless and it had quite an effect on me. Up until this point Barb and myself didn't make out that much just a little 'necking, and a little touchy feely. Later after driving around a bit I found a secluded spot and we began some heavy petting in the back seat and then we made love.

Barb was also involved with the 'Windsor Little Theatre' group. She worked off stage, behind the scenes. One night they were doing a production of 'Barefoot in the Park." I wasn't much for the theatre but I went that night for the sole purpose of taking Barb out after the performance. I did watch the play though, and as a result, I am still not much on the theatre. One night, however, Barb suggested that we go to the movies, I wasn't much for movies either but off we went. The movie was 'The Sound of Music' and I enjoyed it immensely. At intermission though, I got up to leave and Barb said, "Where are you going? It isn't over." I didn't realize that it was just the intermission and I happily sat back down and thoroughly enjoyed the rest of the movie. As I had said, I am not much on movies, but Barb introduced me to the best movie that I have ever seen, and I have watched it a number of times since.

The Seed was planted

I GOT A call from Barb one day asking me to come over that night. When I got there Barb and Frieda were sitting on the couch looking kind of sullen. Frieda spoke first. "Barbara went to the doctor today and found out that she's pregnant. What are you going to do about it?"

I was more than a little taken back, but I think I was taken back more because of Frieda's tone when she said, "What are you going to do about it?" I had no intention of skirting my responsibilities; after all, I had already asked her to marry me didn't I? But at that moment I just had to get out of there and go think. So I simply said that I needed a little time to digest this news and that I would talk to Barb soon. Off to the Royal Tavern I went and not just because I lived there, but because I needed a crutch, a crutch which came in the form of beer. Shortly after, I went to my dad's room and made the announcement. "Barbs pregnant!" My dad really liked Barb, he liked her very much, and it didn't take him even one second to respond. "You are going to do the right thing by her. You are going to marry her."

I think what was hitting me the hardest in this last hour or so, wasn't the fact that Barb was pregnant; it was the threatening tone used by both Frieda and my dad. Was I actually perceived to be, so aloof as to the seriousness of this situation and to Barb's feelings as well? Was I actually perceived to be a louse? Well I wasn't, and I can't remember exactly how I handled it with Barb, but I hope that I had asked her to marry me, and didn't simply say, "We are going to get married."

Here we were, Barb, me and baby making three, and we literally didn't have a pot to stew in. We didn't even have a place to live. Good old dad to the rescue. He had a lady friend that had had a bad accident. She was in the hospital, and would be for some time. She had an apartment that she was paying rent for but it was of no use to her at this time. She couldn't give it up because she would need it when she was released from the hospital, and she really didn't want to sub-let to strangers either. We had previously visited her in the hospital with my dad, and so by knowing my dad and having met us, she was only too glad to sub-let the apartment to Barb and myself. We then went to see a minister, whom my family had known for years, but he was away on sabbatical, so we made arrangements with his stand-in Reverend Freak to perform the wedding service. The date was now set. On August 3 1968 we would become Mr. And Mrs. Summers.

August 3 1968

THE DAY BEFORE our wedding Barb and I got the keys to our new apartment, and not even having a can of beans to put on the shelves, we went grocery shopping. We also bought some drinks and snacks for the small reception that we were going to have at Harry and Frieda's house after the wedding. The grocery shopping really opened my eyes to something that I had never really considered before, which was the fact that there were two of us now and we were going to have to eat. Not only that, we were going to have to cook what we ate. Not only that we would have to do this grocery shopping every week. Not only that....and not only that...and not only that...Having finally completed our shopping and parting with all that lovely grocery money, we too parted ways for the night and after we kissed goodbye I thought to myself very soberly, "There would be no more parting ways."

I headed back to the Royal Tavern to get ready for a little stag party that my friends had arranged. I don't remember much about the stag, but I do remember that there were wedding gifts for Barb and me, stored behind the bar. The owner of the Royal, Steve Sukunda, had told me to come to the bar the next morning before opening to collect them.

Saturday morning came and I showered up and went to my sister and brother in-law's house. My brother in-law Hal was to be my best man and my sister Bev would have her hands full at the wedding minding their baby girl Kristen. My purpose there was to wash and wax my car, which I did and I was feeling pretty good too. I actually felt very positive and excited about prospect of getting married and having Mrs. Barbara Summers as my partner in wedlock, and of course, as a matter of fact, I could have sex with Barb anytime I wanted, and not in the back seat of a car. One thing I had to learn though, it wouldn't necessarily be my decision alone, but I would soon learn.

Here comes the Groom

I LEFT BEV and Hal's and headed back to the Royal. It was about 11:00 a.m. and I went to the bar first to get the wedding gifts before getting ready for the wedding. Steve let me in the back door and we walked to the bar. "Have a beer on me Gary" as he started to pour a draft. "No thanks Steve, I'm getting married at two o'clock and I really don't want a beer." "Come on" he said, just one. Besides I want to talk to you," as he placed the beer in front of me. "Okay, just one and then I'm out of here." "Okay" he said and added, "take it from me Gary, you don't really want to get married, believe me." "Yes I do." I said sternly. Steve continued talking and he went on and on about all the negatives of married life and elaborated on all the positives of being single. The beer did taste good so I didn't say no to the second one that he put in front of me.

A few minutes later he said, "Have a shot on me Gary" "No thanks Steve I'd better not." "Come on" he continued, "Just a little Cherry Brandy, it's your favourite" and he placed it in front of me. Good old Steve, he just kept on and on about all the opportunities there were by staying single. Before I knew it, it was opening time and in came all the lunchtime cronies. Within minutes I was bombarded with more of the same jeering that I had endured from Steve and was given more beer as well. About one o'clock in came my dad and Hal and they were livid. "What in the hell are you up too?" My dad asked. I simply replied with a drunken burp, "I've decided that I'm not getting married." Like hell you're not" they said as they carried me out of the Royal and upstairs to my shower. Well, we made it to the church on time and I even felt sober. "That dam Steve." I thought. After all that, our wedding gifts were still behind the bar at the Royal. Oh well, I guess Barb and I will pick them up as man and wife.

I was of course standing at the altar with Hal at my side when Barb, accompanied by organ music, began her walk down the aisle with Harry. Harry was chosen to give her away. As I turned to look at her, that's when it began, the deluge. I have always been an emotional suck, but this time the floodgates of my eyes opened like never before and I was unable to close them. I was a mess. I was really unable to talk other than to offer a sobbing, "I do." It was soon over and Mr. And Mrs. Summers walked down the aisle into the bright sunshine as mouse and wife.

Mr and Mrs Summers
August 3 1968

It wasn't just 'ME' Anymore

AFTER HAVING A few wedding pictures taken at the church and receiving well wishes from our guests, my dad chauffeured us in my convertible to the little reception. We had a little time to put in before getting to Frieda and Harry's, so on the way my dad stopped and parked across the street from a liquor store and asked me to run in and pick him up a Mickey of rye. I thought it was a little strange because there was liquor at the reception, but oh well. Well I was gone, and of course the real reason for my dismissal, was to give my dad a chance to have a few words with Barb. I didn't know this at the time, nor would find out what was said for some years to come. Barb just kept it to herself, just as she has kept so many things to herself throughout our married life especially during difficult Gary times. The little talk certainly wasn't the traditional fatherly in-law advice to a new bride. It was more like giving Barb assurance that she wasn't alone, and that she could go to him at any time for anything that might trouble her. He told Barb that if I ever gave her any problems or hurt her in any way to simply let him know and he would straighten me out promptly.

The honeymoon was short to say the least. As a wedding present my dad had made reservations at the Holiday Inn on the Detroit River complete with dinner and breakfast. Our room was on the first floor and had a balcony overlooking the river. We left the reception and arrived at the hotel coming in from the east. If we had come in from the west, like we were supposed to, we would have seen the hotel's large neon sign which boldly said, "Wedding Congratulations to Barb and Gary." We never did see the sign, but found out about it later. We checked in, and then we went for dinner. After Barb had finished her dinner, in which I merely kept her company because I was too nervous to eat, we retired to our room. We then sat on our balcony for a while; just talking and watching the shimmering ripples of the river go by. It was nice and we were both beginning to relax. Sitting outside, however, proved to be a mistake, which was quickly realized when we entered our room. Barb was completely covered with mosquito bites. What was that about me having sex anytime I wanted to?

The following morning after breakfast we checked into our apartment and then headed for my dad's place. There, with my dad and his lady friend Mil, we played euchre and had KFC for dinner. It was Sunday and because we all had to work the next morning and Barb had to attend school, we made it an early night and off to our new abode we went, mosquito bites and all.

It certainly was different the next day, being married in all. After leaving work, instead of heading to the Royal Tavern for a few beers, I headed home to our apartment and my new wife Barb. Dinner was on the stove, if that's what you called it. I was now going to have to adjust to English cooking. Oh well. Each night was basically the same. We would have dinner and then watch the telly. The weekend came and I'm not sure what we did on the Friday, but after doing groceries the next morning, I took Barb home and told her that I was going over to Bev and Hal's. Barb asked if she was coming with me and I said no because it was just "something that I wanted to do." When I got to their place, they asked where Barb was, so I told them that she was back at the apartment. They couldn't believe their ears, and I couldn't believe their mouths. "What a rotten thing to do. You've only been married for one week and you just dump her at the apartment and leave her all alone? Go get her now!" they yelled. On the way back to the apartment I gave it some thought and came to my senses. I thought to myself: "What the hell was that all about anyway, leaving Barb alone?" In my mind I guess I was just flaunting my right to male freedom and that Barb didn't have to go everywhere with me. Wrong! When I got back to the apartment, Barb was just sitting there and said nothing. I felt so bad. I said, "I'm sorry, that was so stupid and selfish of me, it won't happen again, I promise!" In fact, it never, ever happened again. It was now WE and no more ME. Back to Bev and Hal's we went, together this time, and ended up having a really good time. We also stopped by the Royal on our way home to pick up our wedding gifts. It was different this time though; it was just in and out. Farewell to the bar at the Royal.

Barb and I were now adjusting very nicely to married life, but it wasn't long before we had pull up stakes. The lady, from whom we were subletting the apartment, was getting out of the hospital soon and I had to find us a place to live and fast. Windsor at the time had more of a demand for rental units than there was a supply of them. It was so bad, that people would get the daily newspapers hot off the press and rush to the rental unit that was advertised, only to find a line up. They would then have to go through an interview to even be considered. It was pretty scary times, but as usual, I got lucky and found us a place. It wasn't much of place that's for sure and it makes me shutter as I think about it now, but it was shelter. Thanks again mom!

The apartment was located over a bakery and our unit was on the third story.

We were required to give an advanced deposit plus a month's rent on top of that. We still didn't have a pot to stew in let alone furniture. Thank goodness for financing, however, it was also the beginning of debt. We fixed the place up as nice as we could and lived there reasonably happy, along with our pet cockroaches. It wasn't a desirable neighbourhood either. It only took a couple of days before my battery was stolen from the car. Thank goodness we didn't have to live there for long. Dad came to the rescue again. Through friends, he had found us a duplex house on Moy Ave. It had two bedrooms, which would come in handy when our baby was born; it had a kitchen, dining room, living room and even a front and back yard. We didn't even have to line up for an interview. We simply met the landlord and his wife and it was ours. Things were coming together.

We lived on Moy Ave for about four years, and while living there, Gary Hugh Summers Jr. was born on March 9 1969. A few weeks earlier we were in the final process of making arrangements for Barbs mom and dad to come to Canada for a visit, but suddenly and sadly her father Hugh, passed away. Barb was in no condition, at that time, to fly home so she had to go through her grieving process without her family back in England, but at least I was there for her.

Some months later we arranged for Barb's mother Doris, Barb's Sister Margaret Lucas, and Margaret's daughter Carolyn to come for a visit. It was good for Barb to see her family again and it was also good for me to finally meet my in-laws. We had a good visit and it wasn't long after Doris's return to England that we got a letter from her saying that she wanted to move to Canada and live with us. We agreed to have her, and the long process of her moving to Canada began. When finally, all conditions for her immigration were satisfied, Barb's mom was on her way. The timing of her arrival coincided with the birth of our little girl Victoria Lee Summers. She was born on July 14, 1971.

I have always heard jokes about mother-in laws, but as it turned out with Doris, it was not a joke. I felt that Doris was too set in her ways and she had difficulties adjusting to our way of life, and our way of raising Gary and Vicki. There were many other issues as well, such as poor sleeping conditions because of our hot summer temperatures. It didn't work out and she returned to England.

I strongly believe, and feel badly, that eighty percent of the problem was of course me, 'Mr. Lovable,' however, many years later, my sister and brother-in law; Margaret and Mike Lucas, said that Doris was the very same way with them and that it wasn't necessarily all my fault. She was too set in her ways. That gave me some relief and some closure.

We were now a family of four and finances were tight, and as much as I loved our convertible, it had to go. When I told my father that I was going to sell it, he decided to buy it himself. I don't know if he truly wanted it, or if he was just trying to help us out. As part of the sale, I took the little heap he was driving. It was an ugly Ford Falcon but that was okay because I wasn't out to impress the girls anymore, I only needed to get around.

Most tragically, and not long after our car exchange, my dad was in a serious car accident. He was picking up his friend Mil from her daughter's house, and as he was backing out of the driveway, a car that was travelling at an outrageous speed, and on the wrong side of the road, smashed into my dad's car. The collision literally tore my dad's car in half and most of his scalp as well. The other vehicle still continued on, careening a ditch, knocking down a tree, and travelled another 250 feet before smashing into a house. My dad was rushed to the hospital in critical condition while Mil, who suffered some facial injuries black eyes and bruises, pulled out of it okay. My dad survived but he would never be the same again. The point of impact was just behind the driver's seat and the next day a picture of the convertible was shown on the front page of the Windsor Star. The picture only showed the front end of my dad's car because that's all that was really left of it. It appeared as though it had been cut in half with a hacksaw. The caption said, "Two people actually survived this collision." The driver of the other car did survived as well, although it took the fire department hours to free him. Even though, the police report clearly indicated that alcohol and speed were the contributing factors, my dad's lawyer said that the court case could, and very possibly, take years to settle. About a year later my dad decided to settle out of court. It wasn't a big settlement but it would enable my dad to enjoy his self-chosen life style, living comfortably above the Royal Tavern and simply walking down to the bar for a beer and a bite when he wanted to.

CHAPTER 7

Change was on the Horizon

IN AND OUT of raising a family and working at the power station, I managed to complete a three-year electronic technology program along with various, non-technical collage certificate courses. I was also actively involved as an instructor with the Windsor Sea Cadet Corps, and as well, the Canadian Naval Reserve. This involvement provided a lot of social activity as well. At least once a week besides drill nights, there was always something going on that involved our spouses as well. There were formal dinners; golf tournaments, chess matches and movie nights just to name a few. Barb and I participated in most of these functions and enjoyed them thoroughly.

Around about this time my company Ontario Hydro, Thermal Division, had introduced a new initiative called, 'The Composite Trade Program.' The program was strictly voluntary and was available to anyone who wanted to sign up. It also provided a financial incentive. I liked the whole idea of it so I signed up immediately. Over a two-year period I was to receive, on, and off the job training, to become qualified in a second trade, in my case that would be an instrument technician. In the end I would achieve the status of 'Electrical and Instrument Technician 1' I was the first electrician at our power station to be selected for the offsite training. I had to travel a considerable distance north to a training centre in Orangeville Ontario, which was owned and staffed by Ontario Hydro Personnel. It was called the Ontario Hydro Conference and Development Centre. Electricians from all of the thermal power stations in Ontario Hydro attended this first two-week session.

Upon completing the course, I returned to the power station and was assigned to the instrumentation shop for a period of two weeks. This follow up to the training would serve as a practical, on the job, re-enforcement. I was quite pleased when my foreman Jack Lay handed me my exam results from the C&D Centre and announced that I had received the second highest mark in the class. The results were not the real reason that I was quite pleased, because, and of course, I actually expected to be Numero Uno, but it was Jack himself. He was so proud that an electrician from his shop, and from his small and aging Thermal Power Station, had performed well and achieved high marks. That was Jack. I love the guy.

Soon after the Composite Training Program was introduced, Ontario Hydro, Thermal Division, advertised a job vacancy for an Electrical Instructor. When I saw the advertisement I was instantly intrigued, so I approached Jack to get his opinion as to what he thought it was all about. Having seeing it for the first time, and without giving it much consideration, he merely said that it sounded like an ideal job for a graduate engineer in training. Engineer or not, I applied.

At about the same time that this was happening; I had applied for the 'Officers Candidate

Training School' at *CFRB London*, Ontario. I was accepted and immediately requested a leave of absence from Ontario Hydro to attend. Not only was I granted a leave of absence, but as well, Ontario Hydro would pay me the difference between my minimal reservist pay and my normal Hydro pay. What a company, I love Ontario Hydro. I must qualify at this time that Barb was, and always has been 100% supportive of me pursuing my goals. She has always stood behind me, no matter of uncertainties, which has made a major difference, not only in my life but also in our lives together. I love that girl.

Soon afterward, I was on my way to *CFRB London*; however, it was not without some interim stress. Just a few days prior to my leaving I had received a letter from the Ontario Hydro's Thermal Training Centre (TTC). The letter requested me to attend an interview at the TTC's temporary location at the R.L. Hearn Generating Station in Toronto. The interview was scheduled on a day that happened to coincide with my military leave of absence. I scrambled to work things out and in the end, and thanks to my Commanding Officer, I was granted permission to attend the interview during my training but on condition that I make up for the lost time. No problem!

I arrived at the Canadian Forces base in London and was assigned my quarters or I should say barracks. It was late at night, so I basically organized my belongings, had a brief chat with some of my Bunkie's, and hit the sack. Very early the next morning, memories of my first morning at the U.S. Naval Boot Camp in San Diego California came back in a flash. There was someone banging and yelling at us to hit the deck and get our butts in gear. During these few moments of hearing derogatory comments, something stood out to me that was considerably different from that first morning at boot camp, besides the fact that strong foul language was not used; every order was followed by the plural word "Sirs."

It was during the second week of my training at *CFRB London* that I headed for Toronto to attend my interview. During the trip I didn't really have time to get nervous about the interview because all of my nerves were used up just getting through Toronto and trying to find the R.L. Hearn Generating Station. I finally arrived and I arrived on time. The newly formed 'Thermal Training Centre' was temporarily located in portable trailers adjacent to the generating station. Senior Training Officer, Hank Stassen, along with Roger Cornell the Personnel Officer conducted the first half of the interview, which was basically technical. The Manager of Training, Mr. Jack Savoury joined in during the second half, which was basically personal. This part of the interview gave them the opportunity to find out who Gary Summers really was. Jack Savoury led off the questioning by asking if I had any instructional experience. I explained my previous experiences in the U.S.N; and that I was presently attending the Reserve Officers Training Program at CFRB London, of which, I had just completed the Canadian Military Instructional Techniques Course. He seemed genuinely interested in my military background, which put me more at ease during the rest of the interview. Upon completing the interview they thanked me for attending, and explained that they had many more interviews to conduct before making their final decision. I headed back to *CFRB London* feeling pretty good, but at the same time, I felt that even being considered for the Instructor's position was very remote indeed.

After completing our training program at *CFRB London* our graduating class of 'Sir's' celebrated with a semi-formal dinner and a party. The following morning after breakfast, I was heading to my barracks to pack up and head home, when I heard a sweet voice from above saying, "Hi Gary." Looking back now, I don't have a lot of memories of *CFRB London,* but I have maintained this one memory. The young lady, a fellow 'Sir' explained that she was waiting for her husband to pick her up and take her home. Her barracks was empty, because all of the other 'Her' 'Sir's' had left earlier. She was a most beautiful 'Sir' and had a figure to match. It wasn't so much that she had asked me to come up to her room and keep her company, but it was the sultry way in which she had asked me. She said it in such a suggestive way that I thought she was inviting me up for much more. The temptation was great, and it was with great difficulty that I declined. I faithfully returned home to Barb. I did, however, bring home a lasting fantasy.

I returned home to our hole in the wall, literally. While I was in London, there had been a water leak in the pipes of the upstairs unit, and it had seeped down through our walls and into the dining room. Contractors had been in to rip the wall apart and repair the pipe, which they did, but the hole was still there. It was a mess. Barb had a bad week, with being all alone, and caring for our two little ones, and on top of that, strangers were in the house banging away causing dust to fly all over. She was a little strained. Things were okay now though, because I was home.

I returned to work on Monday and everything got back to normal, except that we still had the hole in the wall. The following week, Jack handed me a letter that was sent from the 'Thermal Training Centre.' I opened it anticipating a Dear John letter, but it wasn't. I couldn't believe my eyes when I read. "I am pleased to inform you that you have been selected as an Electrical Instructor in the.......Yah Hoo! I got the job. I immediately called Barb with the news and told her that we would soon be moving to Toronto. Although the hole in our wall hadn't been repaired yet, Barb was in the process of doing so, and painting a wall in the hallway, which had received some damage from the contractor work. After hearing my good news, she thought to herself, "the heck with finishing this job." She did finish painting the wall though.

Farewell Windsor

THE OFFER LETTER that I received from the TTC was dated August 6, 1974. Barb and I had celebrated our 6th wedding anniversary just three days prior, not realizing that a wonderful anniversary present was in the mail. There was some urgency on the part of the TTC to get me on board as soon as possible, but there was reluctance from my station to release me until they could find a replacement, claiming that they couldn't afford to let me go. I knew what the shop's workload was and I also knew that I was expendable. So, 'Lovable' me took a week off to prove my point. Point taken and my starting date in Toronto was the day after Labour Day

September 2, 1974. With only a couple of weeks until I had to report to the training centre, there was, to say the least, a flurry of activity in our house. Arrangements were made through the TTC to have our household effects packed and transported to our new residence, which turned out to be the city of Burlington.

Immediately after I had accepted the position of Instructor, I had received some advice from a Senior Training Officer there, suggesting that I move to Burlington and commute to Toronto. The reason being was based upon rumour that the permanent Thermal Training Centre would be built west of Toronto close to Burlington. That Training Officer whose name was Robert lived there as well. With only two weeks to go I had to scramble to find a place to live. It turns out that an English couple, which Barb had known before meeting me, lived in Burlington. Their name was Brian and Mildred. He worked for Bell Canada in Windsor and was transferred to Burlington about a year earlier. We made contact with them and explained our dire situation. They were only too happy to search for a suitable place for us to live, and asked us to come and stay with them the following weekend. Off to Burlington we went, and with only one week to go, we signed a lease on a townhouse that Brian and Mildred had found for us. It was ideal, and among many amenities that Barb and I liked, it had a swimming pool. Strangely enough though, our son Gary was more excited about something else. It had two bathrooms. When we returned to Windsor, that's all that Gary talked about, and to everyone, "It has two bathrooms!"

I was excited that we finally had an address, Barb was excited to leave that hole in the wall, and I don't really know if our two year old Vicki was excited about anything. The movers came on a Wednesday to pack our belongings and loaded the truck Thursday. We would meet them in Burlington on Saturday morning.

That night, after a farewell get together with our family, we checked into the Holiday Inn. It was the same hotel that we had stayed on our honeymoon night, only now there were four of us. We retired early because of the long drive ahead of us the following morning. As I lay in bed, trying to get to sleep, I began to think of what lay ahead of us. Because of the suddenness of this move, and all the frantic preparations involved, it was really the first time I had to give it some serious thought. The more I thought, the more insecure I felt. I was all alone. There would be no family or friends nearby to lend a helping hand when needed. I had a wife and two children to support, and I was leaving a job in which I felt completely secure. I was actually feeling that I had absolutely no control in what had happened, or what was going to happen. Everything leading up to this moment had been controlled, and not by me. I prayed to my mom for strength and cried myself to sleep.

CHAPTER 8

The Thermal Training Centre

WE LEFT WINDSOR the next morning and I was feeling much better and more secure. In fact I was pumped up and was ready for what lay ahead. We had pre-booked a room at the Holiday Inn in Hamilton, which is just on the outskirts of Burlington and only a matter of minutes to our townhouse.

That night we treated Brian and Mildred to dinner just as a small thanks to for finding a place for us to live. On Saturday morning everything went according to plan. The moving truck arrived on time and while they unloaded, I went looking for a beer store, so the movers could have a cool one when the job was done. When I returned, Mildred took Barb grocery shopping,

Gary played musical toilets, and I have no idea what Vicki did?

On Sunday we all went for a swim in the pool. It was a whole new life.

I must mention that a couple of years before, I had been looking to buy a car, as the one I as driving expired itself, so I found a 1965 Thunderbird convertible listed in the newspaper for an unbelievably low price. The guy that was selling it was a university student and he needed the money. Another reason for the low price was that the convertible top did not work. It was the classic T-bird convertible and to me, it was an engineering marvel. If the top had worked, and was to be lowered, it would automatically unscrew itself from the windshield frame. At the same time, the trunk lid would automatically unscrewed itself from behind the rear seat, which would then open, allowing the convertible top to fold into the trunk. The trunk lid then lowered and screwed itself back in behind the rear seat. Working or not I bought it in a flash. After getting it home it was a matter of minutes for me to find the problem. It was, as I figured, an open circuit, in which I quickly corrected. I had myself a wonderful car and enjoyed it thoroughly.

On Labour Day, the day before my first day on the job as an instructor, I made a trial run to Toronto just to make sure that I knew the way. I also wanted to determine how long the trip would take. The trip was a snap and it only took about forty minutes each way. It was a nice day and I had the top down. When I returned to our town house, the convertible top wouldn't go up. I panicked! I had just heard on the radio that rain was forecast for overnight and throughout the next day. I just pictured myself showing up for work on my first day, soaking wet from sitting in my bathtub car. I didn't have the time or the tools to troubleshoot, but I did somehow, manage to disconnect the hydraulics and get the convertible top closed manually.

The next morning, dressed in my best suit and looking good, I left home an hour and a half early, and headed to Toronto. When I got on the QEW my first thought was; "Where in the hell did all this traffic come from." I was listening to the radio as I crept along and found out that TTC was on strike. Not the TTC that I was heading for, but it was a Toronto Transit Commission strike, and there were no buses, subways or trains, just a billion cars all around me and all heading in the same direction. In an instant I had a bad case of traffic phobia. I began to worry that I might be late for work, and on my first day! So much for yesterday's trial run. A little further down the road, a radio station D.J. interrupted my panic with this announcement, "We would like to welcome Gary Summers back to Toronto." I thought to myself, "What a nice city, I was only in Toronto once before, and that had been for my interview a month earlier, and now they are welcoming me back." It turned out that the Gary Summers being welcomed back was a sports caster who been away from the station for a while. Oh well, at least it made me smile.

Just before my starting time of eight o'clock, I arrived, stressed out, but I arrived. The first person to greet me as I entered a trailer was the manager Jack Savoury. I don't know which way he came to work, but the first words that came out of my mouth were: "I have never driven through anything like that before in my entire life." Jack merely chuckled and welcomed me aboard. There were a few staff members late for work that day; one of them was Robert, Senior Training Officer who had recommended that I move to Burlington. Later in the day, I found out that he lived only a couple of blocks from my townhouse, so he suggested that we car pool.

Senior Training Officer Hank Stassen, who headed up my interview four weeks prior, was now my supervisor. He was an absolute gentleman, and I instantly liked and respected him. There were three trailers at the time, one being the main office, were senior management and the clerical staff were located, the other was the office were I would work, and the third was used as a training classroom. Until the permanent site for TTC was established, our technical training would be conducted at the Conference and Development Centre in Orangeville. It was at this location that I would spend a considerable amount of time. We also utilized Humber Collage of Applied Arts and Sciences for some of our basic technical training;

Hank took me around and introduced me to all staff members. Like myself, the entire staff had been recently appointed to their new positions, and we were now the pioneers of the Thermal Training Centre. I was pretty impressed with everyone. In the main trailer there was Connie, and Penny who ran the office, Accountant Bob, Manager Jack, Senior Training Officer Robert, Training Officers, Mel (Operations) and Mike (Instrumentation.)

Located in my trailer, were Senior Training Officer, Hank, Assistant Training Officers, Larry (Electrical) and Bill, (Operations.) There was only one other instructor besides me at that time and his name was Brian, a mechanical instructor.

There were also two part time members of the training staff, Ed (Training and Recruitment Officer) and Roger (Personnel Officer) both being enlisted when their services were required from their regular work locations at head office.

After the introductions, Hank showed me to my work area. I put my not so heavy, brand-new briefcase on my desk. Brand-new, because it was my going away gift from my friends at the Keith Station, and not so heavy, because I only had a sandwich in it. I then sat at my desk; looked at my phone and called Jack Lay just to say hi. I don't recall much more about that first day other than feeling very excited about this new world I had just entered. Even the two hours that it took me to get home didn't bother me very much because I was filled with so many nice thoughts. Barb was equally happy when I got home, not so much that I was home, but this was the first time that she had a washer and dryer. For the four years that we lived on Moy Ave; she washed cloths using an old-fashioned ringer washing machine, and dried them on a clothes line outside in the summer and on a basement cloths line in the winter. We were moving on up.

Life in the Slow Lane

MY SECOND DAY on the job began with a brief walk over to Roberts's house where he would then drive us to work. My briefcase seemed a little heavier than on the first day, probably because Barb added an extra sandwich to my lunch. The transit strike was still on so Robert had suggested that we leave about fifteen minutes earlier than his normal departure time. Robert's normal departure time however, would prove difficult for me to adjust to, because I had always been an early bird, and usually arrived at work no less than a half hour early. If I was driving alone, and knowing about the TTC strike, I would have left Burlington a lot earlier and would have been at work about the same time that we were about to leave. The following day it was my turn to drive. The strike was over so the QEW flowed fairly well. During the drive, the T-bird started doing a little Elvis impersonation. It was shaking, rattling and rolling. It handled better at lower speeds, so lower speeds we did. I took it to a service centre when I got home that night only to find out that the work that was supposed to have been done before we left Windsor, never was. Besides the suspension, there were other problems as well. The mechanic who did the work in Windsor knew that I was moving to Toronto, and he probably just made a few temporary adjustments, charging me the full cost of replacement. I had been ripped off.

Within a few days I found a certified used car for sale. The person selling it was a schoolteacher and the price was right. He was not interested in a trade- in at all. I explained to him that I didn't have the time, or the money, to restore it myself, but if he did, he could make a good turn-over profit. He didn't want it. Besides being upset about having been ripped off, I was in a predicament were I desperately needed a reliable car, especially with the all travelling I was going to be doing. I really didn't have a place to keep it either. In the end, a deal was made. I bought his certified 1965 Ford Fairlane, and he in turn, bought the T-bird for a mere dollar. I was desperate and had little choice, but I would always regret getting rid of that beautiful bird.

Let the Training Begin

I SPENT THE second and third week of my new job attending an Instructional Techniques Workshop in Orangeville. Ed Weib was one of the facilitators. It was a very dynamic and enjoyable workshop, and Ed was an exceptional trainer. Some of Ed's personal, presentation techniques impressed me so much that I integrated them with my own techniques, and have used them throughout my entire career.

The motif of this work shop, and what we would take away with us, as part of our professional repertoire, was the methodology of measurable, performance based training. Near the end of our first week, we were given an assignment to deliver a forty five minute training presentation the following Friday. The subject matter was our choice, and we were required to develop a lesson plan, training objectives, and the criterion. We would prepare and make use of all the audio and visual training aids available to us. Our presentations would be videotaped for the purpose of critiquing. I chose for my subject, a favorite pastime of mine, the game of chess.

My objective, at the end of my forty five minute presentation, was to have participants, who had never played the game before, competently play a game of chess, while knowing all the rules, moves and terminal objective associated with it. I could not, and did not, expect a check mate, within the time span given, however, by empowering the participants with the knowledge, strategies and objective of the game, a check mate, or at least a draw, would be inevitable. When I submitted to the facilitators what my objective was, I was cautioned that I might be biting off a little more than I could chew given the time constraint.

By the end of the first week, I was totally motivated and spent the entire weekend designing and developing my presentation, and of course, the training aids that I would use. At eleven o'clock on the Friday of the following week, I began my presentation. It was successful beyond my expectations. I enjoyed my first success as an instructor and it felt good. There actually was a check mate, but it wasn't by the end of my presentation, the participants wouldn't stop playing and continued on during lunch. They were hungry but it wasn't for food.

As far as the taping of my presentation, there wasn't much critiquing other than, as it was pointed out to me by the facilitators, I had, and still have a weak right, which means I tend to talk more to the participants to my left and centre, than those to my right. I have done an untold number of presentations in my life, and I still catch myself being weak to the right, but thanks to that workshop many years ago, I always control it.

When viewing the videotape, however, there was something else that stood out to me, as well as others, and it was something I had never realized before. I not only looked like the comedian Bob Newhart, but I had the same mannerisms and gestures. In fact, one time when I was at Canada's Wonderland, a young lad and his father approached me and asked me for an autograph. Sorry Bob, but I couldn't say no. Even recently, while flying to the Caribbean and seated in first class, the entire crew thought I looked like Bob Newhart. I guess I'm aging like him as well. No offence Bob, but I'd rather be identified with Tom Cruise.

Unexpected Feeling

WHEN I RETURNED to the TTC after completing the Instructional Techniques Workshop, I was asked by my supervisor Hank, if I would like to go on a two day trip to the Keith station in Windsor and then on to the Lambton station in Sarnia. If so, I would be picked up the next morning by two people from Head Office. The purpose of the trip was to interview electrical apprentices in order to monitor and assess their on-the-job training progress.

Up until the TTC was formed, all training for Thermal Generation Personnel was conducted at the C&D Centre in Orangeville, and was coordinated by a group of specialists working out of Head Office. Our newly formed training centre was in the transition of taking over all training responsibilities from the C&D Centre and Head office. I myself, being in a developmental transition, jumped at the chance to go.

I was picked up the next morning by Robert, who was a veteran training specialist and Clive, an electrical engineer who was new to the company and had recently been appointed to the position of Departmental Superintendant. I felt proud to be traveling in such esteemed company.

I had just transferred from the Keith Station a few weeks ago, and as I think back now, I was too vainly excited about the prospect of returning. There, I was the conquering hero, returning to the troops in his new role as instructor, dressed in suit and tie, being accompanied by professionals from Head Office and impressing everyone. Yah right!

The interviews with the apprentices had been prescheduled, so we got right to work, although I was just basically sitting in, having little input. During the interview, I wanted to impress everyone with being profound and getting to the core issues of reality, and how an apprentice feels at times. It was a little difficult for me, because two of the apprentices had, at times, been under my wing. Already knowing there on the job performance, I was able to key in on some of their obstacles and pet peeves, such as being treated from time to time, as Gofers.

"When we finished the interviews there wasn't a lot of time left to walk around the station, which I was hoping to do, but I did manage to visit the electrical shop and see my mentor, Jack Lay. It also happened to be coffee break time, so I was able to shoot the breeze for a few minutes with most of my friends and of course, take some ribbing which I truly deserved. This brief get together gave me a very warm and fuzzy feeling. I would have loved to have stayed longer, but we had to travel on to Sarnia where we would check into a hotel for the night. When we drove away from the station, a much unexpected feeling came over me. I suddenly became

depressed. I was picturing the guys in the shop finishing their day and heading home to their families, or as I probably would have, stopping off at the pub down the road for a couple of beers first. Bad me. I felt strangely alone, empty and insecure. Would I rather be back at my old job, or heading off to a hotel in Sarnia? At that moment it was the former. Alas!

The next morning we checked out of the hotel and checked into the Lambton generating station. We only had a few interviews, so we were able to head home in the afternoon. If anything, this trip served as an introduction to the inner workings of the training system, and to meet some trainees, as well as their supervisors. During our drive home I started to feel better. I felt less insecure about myself and much more positive about my new job. Upon arriving home after our long drive and being greeted by my family, I felt completely secure, totally positive, and extremely happy. My past life as an electrician at the Keith station was behind me, and I would never in my working career or travels, feel insecure again.

It wasn't very long after this trip to the Keith Station, that Ontario Hydro released a statement that the Keith Plant in Windsor would be closing. This was devastating news. Jobs for employees willing to move, would be found at other locations, but for those that weren't willing to move, it would be the pink slip. For people like my ex foreman and mentor Jack Lay, having over twenty years service invested, there was only one option, relocate. More about this later.

A Travelling Trainer

LOOKING BACK AT my first training assignment makes me shudder to think about it. The venue, was our temporary training center, more aptly described as a trailer park, in which we had a trailer set up for class room instruction. My class or *'Target Population'* consisted of Operators-in-Training, who in the end would become 4th class Operating Engineers, and be responsible for the efficient and safe operation of Ontario Hydro's, Generating Stations. But first they had to learn all about batteries and the internal chemical reactions that make them produce voltage. Poor guys, oops.... there was one female, who at that time was a pioneer among women who would follow her into the non-traditional trades. And so it began, four hours of lecture in a stifling, closed in, class room. I did my best to make my presentation as entertaining as possible, and yet relate all of this theory into as much practical application as I could. I believe that our training objectives at the time were geared more toward the theory required to pass the Provincial Operating Engineers exams, than to the more needed, on-the-job performance requirements, however, in the end we all knew more about batteries than we would have liked to know, unless of course, one of us ended up on the game show 'Jeopardy'.

Upon completing my battery training, I was all charged up for a new challenge, but that new challenge would take place at the C&D Center in Orangeville for a period of two months. Although I would be provided with food and accommodation, there is no way that I could stay away from my family for five days a week, so I decided to commute. A commute, on a good weather day, would take approximately three hours return, but this wasn't a good time of year for good weather, especially in snow belt country. My project would be to oversee the installation of a training simulator. The working simulator was a scaled down version of a typical system found in power plants, containing, pumps, valves, instrumentation, and a motor control center. The system would be controlled with relay logic in which apprentice electricians would be required to wire in the components, using wiring diagrams, and then be given trouble-shooting assignments by their instructor.

I was assigned two, fourth year apprentices to carry out this project. To make our lives a little easier from being away from home for so much, we decided to work an extra four hours on Thursday night so we could leave at lunch on Fridays. This helped a little bit, but to do that, I would have to stay at the center Thursday nights. I got approval from my training center, but I would only be given mileage for two return trips a week. It would still be worth it to be at home at night, so that's what we did, for a little more than two months. Although there were several snow storms during this period I was never late getting to the C&D Center, but getting home on time was a different story. Sometimes I would get home and only get a few hours of sleep before hitting the road again. The project went well, and it was completed pretty much on schedule, and with great relief I returned to the TTC.

Commuting to Toronto was never easy, but it was a snap compared to driving to Orangeville. When I got back to my office, the place was abuzz with rumours of our new and permanent training center. Some of the powers to be wanted it build near Toronto and others like me wanted it closer to Burlington. The financial justification analysis had begun, as well as the personal politics of location, location, location. This would take a great deal of time, but for the present, we couldn't deliver effective training from a trailer park. Being at the bottom of the Totem pole there would be no input from me. I would just be on the receiving end, and because of the urgency to deliver training, the news I received didn't make me the happiest of campers. I would, in the near future, and for the foreseeable future, deliver trades training at the C&D Center in Orangeville. On the plus side, I wouldn't be assigned there permanently; I would deliver training in two week blocks, and work out of the TTC for two or more weeks in between. I could handle this. So for two years, off and on, this is what I would do.

Trades Training

AS MENTIONED BEFORE, the Thermal Generation Division was heavily involved in establishing composite trades. In the beginning the program was voluntary. The concept was to train and develop trade personnel to at least an 80% level of competency in an associated trade. It was a win-win situation, more money in the pockets of the trade's people, and a more as-needed labour resource for the company.

This would have a large impact on all of us at the TTC, not to mention locating appropriate training facilities until our permanent training center was built. We negotiated a deal with a local community college to provide mechanically related training as well as some basic instrumentation training. We also had to bring the college instructors up to speed as to what our particular training requirements and standards were and of course hire more staff at the TTC. It was busy times.

Besides my own training work load, I was involved in monitoring the quality of training at the community college. My training involvement at the C&D Center, besides the ongoing apprenticeship program, would now include electrical training for instrumentation technicians. In the end, although experiencing many growing pains, the composite trade program was a success, and as a result, my instructional skills and knowledge were fast tracked to a high level of competence.

The New 'Temporary' Thermal Training Center

DURING MY 'ON again, off again' absence from the TTC, negotiations for our new and permanent training center was going very slow. As a result, and because we were in dire need of a training facility, a decision was made to rent a building that would suit our requirements. Within a short time, we found and rented an old and vacant WW11 munitions factory located at the foot of Dixie Road and Lakeshore, in Mississauga. The good news for some of us was that it was closer to home and would drastically cut down our commute time. When I first started at the TTC, and was commuting to Toronto, Robert suggested that we take turns driving. I tried it for a while, but it didn't suit my morning habits. I have always been an early bird, and always showed up for work early, most often, an hour early, and this was even after stopping for a coffee and reading the newspaper. Leaving early also beats the rush hour traffic, so I made the decision to drive alone. This did not sit well with Robert and he never forgot it. He was in a position to make life miserable for me and he did. There would be no advancement in the hierarchy for me, not while he was at the TTC, no matter how good my work performance. Some months later however, he was suddenly replaced, and sent to a new work location. Oh, the power of reasonable prayer. Life at the TTC became very good.

For some months to come, the TTC was a hive of activity. Our staff tripled, our training facilities were becoming well equipped, and we were becoming less dependent on the use of the C&D Center and the local community college.

On The Home Front

IN THE MEAN time, with all that was going on at TTC, life was good at home; we loved Burlington and our town house complex. We had made a lot of good friends and enjoyed our social life. It had been some time, however, since we visited our family in Windsor, mainly because of all my travelling, so we arranged for my father to take a train to Burlington for a visit. It was one of the best visits that I have ever had with my dad. We all, totally enjoyed those few days. Unfortunately, this would be the last time I would see my father. A few months later, on January 24th (Barbs birthday) my dad collapsed in his apartment, and died of a massive heart attack. My dad was only 57 years old. After making the necessary arrangements, and leaving Gary Jr, and Vicki with our neighbours, we headed for Windsor early the following morning. On the way, we hit a blinding snow storm that closed down the highway. We were rerouted via a series of back roads and arrived at the funeral home just a few minutes before the service began. I felt bad that my sister, and her husband Hal, had to take care of all the funeral arrangements, but there wasn't much I could do from my end. It was a quiet service, but ended with quite a shock to me. My father in his living will, had made a final request, and the minister read it out loud to the congregation. "Everyone is invited back to the Royal Tavern for food and drinks, compliments of my son Gary." Thanks dad that was a good one. These were the days of cash, not debit or credit cards, and I really didn't have that much cash, but off to the Royal Tavern we went, and somehow, probably with the help of my brother-in-law, managed to cover the cost of my dad's final request.

My dad was now reunited with my mom, and although there was two years of separation during their marriage, I believe that he truly and always loved her. The loss of my dad however, did not complicate my quest for, my answer 2 a question.

A couple of months after my father's funeral, lightening stuck again, we received word that my uncle Pete passed away and I was asked to be a pallbearer. Barb received the call on Thursday and was informed that the funeral would be on Saturday. I was in Orangeville at the time, attending a meeting, but was scheduled to return home that night, however, the weather had the final say, because we got hit with a massive snow storm and were snow bound. The storm was a total shock to everyone because it was the beginning of April, and when I had left for Orangeville it was warm with Sunny skies. I was dressed for spring, just wearing a light blue suit, no coat, no gloves and no boots. None of our group was prepared for this. Our cars were completely buried, and it was the following afternoon before we managed to dig and push ourselves out. The road out of Orangeville was in terrible shape so we formed a convoy and headed home. The following morning Barb and I left for my uncle's funeral in Waterloo.

My uncle Pete was actually named Howard Hilborn, but for reasons I never knew he was called Pete. I was second named after him, Gary Howard Summers. He was my hero. He had served in WW II and fought in the bloody battle of Dieppe. During the battle he was wounded and taken prisoner. He remained in a concentration camp until the end of the war. I still have the letters that he had written to my mother while he was imprisoned. He and my mom were very close, as they were the youngest of the Hilborn clan, ironically though, they were first of the clan to depart this life. Pete was survived by his wife Genevieve and seven children. It appears as though, he kept very busy after the war.

I guess Barb and I were a little busy later that year as well; she became pregnant with our third child and with all my time away from home it was decided that she should learn to drive and get her licence. Barb was about seven months pregnant, and had recently passed her driving licence test, even though a wasp was buzzing around her while taking the test. This was some feat, because she feared wasps as much as I feared snakes. We also bought a second car so that she could be more mobile especially in her present state. The day after enjoying a long weekend in June, Barb felt some discomfort, possibly a contraction, so I rushed home and took her to the doctor. He examined her and instructed us to get to the hospital immediately and he would meet us there. Soon after arriving Barb went into labour and there was no sign of the doctor. A doctor on duty took over and rushed her to the delivery room. A baby boy, two months premature, was born, but the attending doctor was completely stunned to realise that Barb was expecting twins, and so were we. There was absolutely no indication of this on her record of treatment, and there was never a hint from her doctor that this was even possible. A second baby boy was born and both were put in incubators and rushed to McMaster hospital in Hamilton. We were all in shock, even the attending doctor; in fact he was downright angry as to why there wasn't even a suggestion on record that Barb could be pregnant with twins. Our family doctor never did show up at the hospital nor did we ever hear from, or see him again.

When I watched our newborns, Robert Scott and David Allen through the glass of the incubator, they looked perfectly normal to me except maybe for being a little small. I was told that the next twenty four hours was critical to their survival, and I was told to go home and let Barb rest, because for the time being there was nothing either of us could do. I was given a phone number to call whenever I wanted to check the progress of the twins. So I went home, picked up Gary and Vicki, and made phone calls to all concerned explaining what had happened. About eight p.m. I called the hospital to see how the babies were doing, and was told that the first born, Robert Scott was doing really well and basically out of danger, but David Allen remained a concern. I phoned Barb and told her that things seemed to be ok.

She sounded very relieved and very tired and so was I. It was a long, turbulent day so after Gary and Vicki were asleep I went to bed. The phone rang at 11:00 p.m. It was McMaster hospital informing me that the twins did not survive. I felt like I woke up and entered a nightmare. I told the caller that this was hard to believe because just a few hours earlier I was told that the first born was basically out of danger, and that the situation of the second born didn't seem terribly bad. The caller in a rather loud and angry voice said "who the heck told you that, neither one of them, was never, even close to being out of trouble. I blew up. I have no remembrance to what I actually said, but it was something in regards to the total incompetence of the entire medical profession that day, and slammed down the phone. Now I had to break the news to Barb and that hurt deep.

The next morning after informing all concerned, I called a funeral parlour and set up an appointment for later that day, and then I went to visit Barb. One of the first things that she said was "I'm going to have my tubes tied, no more children." Both, I and her, new doctor suggested that she shouldn't be too hasty in making this important decision, but allow time for the mental healing process. Her mind was made up, however, and there was nothing that was going to change it, and nothing did change it.

Later that day I met with the funeral director and explained the situation. He was a fair man, and volunteered that there should be no reason why both babies couldn't share one coffin. This would certainly relieve the financial burden, so we made the final arrangements. Barb and I agreed that it would be a very quick and simple burial, and that only I would be in attendance, as well as the funeral director and a rep from the cemetery. Barb was still in the hospital. When the little service was completed and I was writing the final cheque on the hood of my car, the damn cemetery rep found out that there were two babies in the coffin, and demanded that the cost be doubled. I could not believe what was happening. In the end the funeral director won out and the entire, sickening situation was put to rest.

Gas Turbines

AFTER THE LOSS of my father, uncle and our twins in such a short period of time, Barb and I had to regroup, refocus and get on with our lives and my career. Back at work, my boss Hank Stassen, informed me that there was going to be a one week Gas Turbine course conducted at the Lennox Generating Station near Kingston. He suggested that I attend as a representative of the TTC. I jumped at the chance. Gas turbines more commonly referred to as jet engines, were installed at all generating stations throughout the province. Their purpose was to supply emergency power to each station in the event of a blackout. Ten years prior while I was in the navy there was a massive blackout that affected the entire north eastern sections of Canada and the United States. It was caused by the failure a simple electromagnetic relay in an Ontario Hydro circuit breaker, which caused a catastrophic domino effect. Something that should never have happened, did happen. Put simply, our thermal power plants tripped off line and were unable to sustain themselves so they shut down. Again, trying to keep it simple, our power plant generators are driven by steam, which is produced by massive high pressure boilers. These boilers are provided with water by massive boiler feed pumps. If the boiler feed pumps could have maintained their operation during the black out, they would have been able to maintain the boiler steam supply to the turbines that drive the generators, which would have resulted in a less catastrophic black out and certainly would have lessened the length of the black out.

The Keith GS, Lambton GS, Nanticoke GS, Lakeview GS and the Hearn GS all had dual shaft, Orenda gas turbines installed for the purpose as was explained above. The Lennox GS, used primarily as a peaking station (not on-line all the time, but used when power demands were high) had single shaft, Solar Turbines installed. These were smaller gas turbines and used only for safe shut down of the station in the event of a blackout. The Thunder Bay GS used Rolls Royce gas turbines. When these units were first installed, manufacturer training was provided, unfortunately, only management personnel were scheduled for this training and in most cases, technical information stopped there.

When I worked at the Keith station, there were many times that gas turbine problems arose, and like myself, no one in our crew had a clue as to how to trouble shoot them. They had complex systems that we were not privy to because of our lack of training. Jack Lay however, had been trained on these units and was the resident expert, but that wasn't much help to me when something went wrong during a black start test at two o'clock in the morning.

So off I went to Kinston and the Lennox GS, for gas turbine training. The instructor was good, and from my prospective it was because he had started his career with the Solar Gas Turbine manufacturer on the shop floor, and worked his way through the company ranks to become their senior trainer. The course was excellent, but once again, other than me, the participants were middle management and not the trade's people who really needed it. Upon completing the course I returned home pumped up and motivated, not necessarily because of the course but what I was going to propose when I got back to work.

My proposal, to the powers that be at the TTC, was to develop a one week Orenda Gas Turbine course. Our four year electrical apprenticeship training program was currently under review with the purpose of eliminating outdated material and replacing it with new and relevant technology. Initially my proposal was rejected, mainly because of one short sighted individual who found it easier to say no than to look at the bigger picture. The bigger picture being, gas turbine generation units are just miniature power plants. They contain all of the electrical systems and components that are relevant throughout the four year apprentice, training program. The operation of a gas turbine is controlled by relay logic (later converted to Programmable Logic Controls) which affords the perfect and realistic opportunity for print reading and actual trouble-shooting tasks. The units consist of AC and DC equipment, instrumentation, inverters, converters, batteries, motor control, metering, oil systems, fuel systems, brush gear.....I could go on and on. Besides fitting perfectly into the 4th year program, it offered a spin off benefit, by providing the stations with some expertise in maintaining and trouble-shooting these units. I had no doubt that this was a win-win situation in every way.

It was a struggle, but in the end it was approved, and I began the course development, but I was going to need a technical advisor and the perfect person was my idol, Mr Jack Lay.

After the Keith Plant was shut down and put in moth balls, Jack Lay was transferred to the Nanticoke GS as an electrical supervisor and was assigned to the project section. When I called him and told him about my developing a GT course, he thought that it was an excellent idea and long overdue. I asked if he would be interested in being a part time technical advisor. He was all for it, but first, we had to get the stations permission to free him up from time to time. Permission granted. Mission accomplished!

When I began the course development, I did so in the same way that I always did and would always do,; start from the thing that's suppose to happen and work backwards. Example, the gas turbine is running, now how did it get that way. Over the years I have preached this to hundreds of trainee's especially when reading an electrical diagram. I also approach the course development from the eyes of a complete novice, I never assume that a trainees' basic knowledge of a subject is a given. After a number of weeks of liaisons with Jack Lay at Nanticoke, and developing the course at TTC, we were finally ready to break a leg. Jack sat in on the first session which was not only filled with challenging practical projects and research, but we were also given permission to use the nearby Lakeview GS gas turbines as needed. We would take out work protection on the units for our physical inspections, identifying system components, tracing oil and fuel systems, etc. I would put actual and realistic faults on the system for the apprentices to trouble-shoot. We would run the units, synchronize, load to peak and shut down. Lakeview received a spin off benefit from this as well, because we would identify systems or components that required attention. In fact when we first started to use these gas turbines, Lakeview's start up reliability was one of the worst in the Province. With our involvement, over time, and our recommendations, Lakeview gas turbines became the most reliable units in the system.

Our first course turned out to be a success, more so than I had hoped for, and within a short period of time, there were constant requests from all over the province for this training. Over the years, I not only delivered training to qualified journeymen, technicians, and engineers, but I also developed and delivered training for operators and mechanical personnel. I soon became the go to guy for technical assistance; even the gas turbine experts (engineers) at head office used me as their consultant. I would say that 98% of the time, I solved gas turbine problems over the phone and usually within minutes. I got to the point where I felt that there was nothing

I didn't know these units. Jack and I stayed in touch over the years, not just sharing technical information but on a personal level as well. He was after all, my mentor.

CHAPTER 9

New Home, New Club

A FEW MONTHS after my father passed away, my sister called to inform me that our father had left us some money and that we were to meet with a lawyer in Windsor to finalize our inheritance. It was to be a quick, in and out meeting, so I decided to take a day off and travel to Windsor by myself. I forget the exact amount that my dad had left me, but Barb and I decided to use it for a down payment on a brand-new townhouse. The timing worked out great as far as our present lease because it was about to expire. We soon moved into our first home on Tyandaga Rd in Burlington. Thanks dad. At about the same time, I had joined the Cedar Springs Racquet Club not far from home. I had always enjoyed the game of tennis but when I joined the club I became totally hooked, almost to the point of obsession. I started off, by playing at the bottom of the C level, and soon won my way up the ladder, through the B and finally becoming an A player. I actually qualified to play a match with Pierre La Marsh our club pro and past Canadian champion. There is no way I could beat him, but I was honoured just to be able to play him. I think Barb, myself and our kids spent every weekend at the club. We made a lot of friends including the club owner Vick Mancini.

Barb and I were now socializing with a completely different class of people than we were accustomed, and we truly enjoyed our new-found, upper crust friends. There were lawyers, doctors, business people, politicians and company managers. There was one noted sports star that I really took to, and that was Tony Gabriel of the CFL, Ottawa Rough Riders. One day, owner Vick Mancini introduced me to Tony and asked me to take him under my wing, and give him tennis lessons. Tony had been named to the Super Star Sports Challenge. Superstars from all Canadian professional sporting teams, chosen for this challenge, were given a month or so to prepare their selves to play in a sport that they had never played. Tony picked tennis. After Tony and I discussed our schedules, and booked advanced court times, I headed home, but as I was leaving I asked Tony if it would be possible, sometime, to get an autographed picture of him for my son Gary Jr.

. He simply said 'no problem'. Within 3 days and before I saw Tony again, my son received a large brown envelope in the mail. It contained not only an autograph picture of Tony Gabriel, but a number of action pictures including an autographed team picture. Although I had only met with him briefly, I guessed that he must have gone to the reception desk at the club to get my home address. What a guy! It was a real pleasure playing with Tony, and it was soon apparent what a natural athlete he was, especially his hand, to eye, to ball, coordination. My most memorable association with Tony was at a fund raising event the club held to support our junior players. Participants in this event, solicited pledges in support of them playing in a twelve hour marathon. The rules allowed a ten minute break every hour, but to me that is not a marathon. A marathon is a marathon and there was no way I was going to take a break and I didn't. I played opponent after opponent for the full 12 hours and at one point, about 4:00 am, I looked up through the club house window and saw Tony, the super star, lying on a couch enjoying his ten minute break. I thought 'who's the super star now?' I ribbed him about this for a while. When the marathon finished and with my feet raw and bleeding I headed for the club house and was quite surprised at my reception. I was given a standing ovation. I hadn't really broadcast that I was going to play without a break, but I guess it was obvious to everyone else. I modestly accepted the applause and said; that because the court time was donated for this event, I wasn't going to waste one minute of free playing time.

Club owner, Vic Mancini and I became good friends. I really enjoyed being with Vic. He not only had a great sense of humour, but there was a certain charisma about him that drew me like a magnet. He drove a pink Rolls Royce at the time, why pink, I have no idea. We both loved playing chess and we played often, sometimes for fifty dollars a game. I really couldn't afford to play for that kind of money, but because of my prowess at playing the game I couldn't refuse. After beating him the first few times, I offered to play one rook short. He accepted and I still kept winning.

When I first joined the club, there were rumours that Vic was linked to the mafia, but this didn't bother me, nor did it mean anything to me. I just didn't care. I also heard at the club that he was currently on trial for tax evasion. The trial was in Hamilton and there were daily updates in the local paper. One afternoon, I stopped off at the club on my way home from work and heard one of the members describe the news event of the day. He said that as Vic Mancini was addressing the judge he did so by speaking with a broad, broken Italian accent. He said "You honah, I dunt know about- a taxa things. My wife a-do the books. She dunt know about -a tax tings' eeder. What am I gonna do, fire my wife a?" Everyone in the club was roaring as the story continued on. The prosecutor interrupted to address the judge and said "Your honour, Vic Mancini was born and raised right here in Hamilton and can speak perfect English. He also knows full well the laws concerning the paying of income taxes." There were a lot of laughs that afternoon at the club, but in court Vic wasn't laughing. He was found guilty and apparently received heavy fines. I never did find out any of the details because like I said, I just didn't care, but it was an enjoyable story.

Barb and I were often invited to Vic's private parties, and on one such occasion, a group of men came in that I had never seen before. A friend told me that it was Johnny Papalia also known as Johnny Pops, a mafia boss. I had never heard of the guy, probably because I was new to the area, but it seemed like everyone else knew about him. When we were seated for dinner, it just happened to be directly across the table from Johnny and his entourage. It didn't bother me, but it seemed to bother Barb. At one point during the night she was staring under the table, so I asked her what she was looking for, replying she said "I'm looking for a place to dive if shooting starts." I laughed and said, "They don't do that kind of thing anymore." I would learn much later in life how naive I really was.

From time to time I would invite friends to the club to either play tennis, or just socialize. One particular Sunday I asked Peter and Susan Uderzal to join Barb and me for a couple of drinks.

Peter had recently joined our staff at the TTC as an Assistant Training Officer, and this was a good opportunity for us to meet each other's spouse and family. After an hour or so at the club we invited them back to our house for dinner, but I had a slight problem, Susan drank rye and coke, and we didn't have any rye. Being a Sunday, the liquor stores were closed so I went to Vic Mancini and asked if I could borrow a bottle from the bar and I would replace it the next day. He said he would like to, but if he got caught doing that, he would lose his liquor licence, so he told me to go to his apartment and his girlfriend would give me a bottle. Barb took Susan home in our car while Peter drove me to the apartment. Vic's girlfriend was a young, beautiful model, and although I had met her before, and had seen her in a TV commercial, I wasn't prepared for seeing as much of her as I did when she opened the door. She wore a simple jeans jacket that was completely unbuttoned in the front and wearing nothing underneath. I was agape, and while thanking her (more for my new fantasy) I took the bottle with shaking hands and returned to the car. I'm glad it wasn't soda pop that I borrowed or the cap would have off. It turned out to be a good Sunday, especially for Susan because it wasn't rye whiskey that Vic gave me it was a forty ounce bottle of Crown Royal. The next day after work, I went to a liquor store to buy a replacement bottle and headed directly to the club. I was taken back a bit, however, when I, and with my deepest thanks, handed the bottle to Vic. He looked at me angrily and said that I had insulted him. The bottle of Crown Royal was intended to be a gift and not to be replaced. I really, really liked Vic Mancini.

New TTC Manager

ONE MORNING, WHILE at work, and somewhat unexpected, it was announced that our manager, Jack Savory was going to retire. His replacement, whom some believed would be Jacks heir apparent, Robert, was not selected, instead he was sent away permanently on some project somewhere. Harry Kirwin became our new manager. Harry was a golden boy in the organization meaning that he was on a fast track through the hierarchy of Ontario Hydro's Thermal Generation Division. Life at TTC became very good indeed. Although Harry was slated for bigger things in the near future, his time at the TTC was momentous to me for a few reasons, but two in particular. Firstly I asked Harry if he would review my personal file because it contained a letter that I did not agree with, and didn't think should be there. He got my file, read the letter and made comment that the person who wrote it sure had it out for me. Then, in front of me, he shredded the letter. I was ecstatic. Secondly, I asked if I was eligible for a paid move from Burlington to Mississauga. The reason being, that when I moved from Windsor, there was a rumour that the permanent TTC would be close to Burlington, so that's why we ended up living there. Now that it seemed likely to be Mississauga, I would like to move closer to work. My paid move, including legal fees, etc; was immediately approved. Again, I was ecstatic.

We had, some months prior, sold our town house in Burlington, and were now renting. At the time of sale, I had thought there was a strong possibility of us moving to South Africa, and I wanted to be ready and available in short notice, but alas that opportunity fell through. Barb and I were now looking to buy a house in Mississauga close to work. My friend and colleague Brian Holtham, was dating a lovely young lady by the name of Helen who had just gotten into the real-estate business. We gave her the particulars of what we were looking for, and what we could afford, (not much) and within a short time she called to say she found something we might like. Like it we did. It was a white, clap board sided, three bedroom bungalow. It had a large detached garage and was situated on a beautiful lot which backed onto a ravine. It had wonderful curb appeal, with a white fenced in front yard, and a huge evergreen tree situated in the far right corner that didn't obstruct the view of the house, or the view of the yard from inside the living room, which had a large picture window. No one was home at the time when we went to check it out, so we could only look through the windows. The site of a wood burning fire place in the living room warmed our thoughts to putting in an offer. Although it was a small house with no basement, only a crawl space, it had a lot of potential. With only a limited view of the house, just by looking through a couple of windows, almost sight unseen, we asked Helen to put in our offer. This was Saturday morning and that night at 5 minutes to twelve, Helen called us and said that the offer was accepted. We now owned a wood burning fire place, sitting in a charming white bungalow, at 1201 Canterbury Avenue, Mississauga. We soon moved into our newly purchased house and began the work required to make it *our* home. The way so many things came together for us and so fast, it left me again thinking that we were not in total control of our destiny. It felt as though this opportunity was prearranged. Thanks mom and dad!

New Jobs

LIFE WAS GOOD on Canterbury Ave; as it was at the TTC. It was great to be just a few minutes from work. I could even go home for lunch. We also lived within three blocks of Lakeshore Blvd, giving us easy access to such things as Canadian tire, a deli, bakery, restaurant and the grocery store A&P. Barb decided one day, that with both kids away at school, and having time on her hands, that she would apply for a job at A&P. It would also bring in extra income that we could surely use. She was accepted and became a cashier. Barb was a dependable and dedicated worker, and because of this, and in a short period of time, a young lady, named Carry, who worked part time as a cashier, asked Barb if she would be interested in working at her mother's motor vehicle licensing office. Carry's mother Jean, interviewed Barb and immediately after, Barb began her new career.

I, myself, after five years of instructing every facet of the Control Maintainer Program, was looking for a change, a new challenge. I was also, at the time, attending night classes at York University. This came about, by the way, as a result of another one of my miracles. I had an intense dream about attending university one night. So much so, that it caused me to bolt upright. It was more like a direction dream, a matter of fact, 'Do it now! Dream. That very morning, I called York University to inquire about enrolment. I couldn't believe my ears when I was told that this was the final day for accepting applications. I applied that day and after having to take an entry test, I was accepted. Thanks again mom and dad!

As I had said, I was looking for a new career challenge, and presto, like magic it was presented to me. Throughout all work locations in Ontario Hydro, there is a system in place to protect workers from harm while performing their work. It's called the "Work Protection Code." (WPC) To the novice, it is extremely complex and requires three days of instruction to qualify and to be able to hold work protection. To the experienced, it requires ongoing vigilance and periodic refresher training. The present instructor of the WPC, Dave Holden, had been selected to oversee the installation and training, of a new computerized operating system at the Lakeview Generating Station, thereby creating a vacancy.

Traditionally, WPC instructors have always been management personnel, although I was not, I was offered the job and proudly took it. For the next few weeks, I sat in on Dave's courses and gradually took over until he deemed me proficient and qualified to solo. I could never completely fill Dave's shoes, as he had a mind of a genius in so many areas, but I would become a Work Protection Code expert and trainer. The one big change that would affect my family life would be the travel. There would be a lot of it.

I totally enjoyed this new job, even the travelling. It gave me the opportunity to visit other cities, generating stations, and meet lots of interesting people. There were times however, that I had to leave home on Sunday afternoons in order to fly to, say Thunder Bay or Atikokan to be ready to deliver a Monday morning workshop. I didn't really mind this. It's just something that you get used to. I was basically my own boss. I did my own scheduling and always did my very best to satisfy all training requests. I hated to say no. I did this job for a couple of years until another very big opportunity presented itself. My career was about to change drastically.

Labour Unrest

IF I REMEMBER correctly, it was early 1985 when talks broke down between union and management. I was a union member at that time and was terrified of going on strike. There were earlier indications that a strike was possible so I made a few financial preparations like selling my motorcycles for example. I had two Hondas both of which I loved, but a strike is a strike and who knew how long it could last. There was an ugly strike years before and it went on for months and months. Some people lost their homes. That wasn't going to happen to me. (I was not affected by that strike thank goodness because I was in a different union.)

I was on my way to work one morning and in doing so I passed the Lakeview Generating Station. My heart sank when I saw picketers blocking the entrance to the station. The strike was on. I continued on to the training centre and met up with my colleagues in the parking lot. We really didn't have union representation or union direction, so we ambled over to a coffee shop to discuss the situation. There was nothing really to discuss because we were on strike, so after a few minutes I headed to the nearest employment office. I didn't care what type of work I got as long as I got work. Within a few minutes I was offered and accepted a job at a fabricating shop. I went home for my safety shoes and was on the job at this sweat shop within an hour of finding out about the strike. It was hard, heavy and somewhat dangerous work but I just hung in there and worked my butt off. I was never one to take coffee breaks or long lunch breaks, so during these times I would just keep myself busy by cleaning equipment, sweeping or garbage detail. Friday came and I learnt that the workers only worked until noon, at which time they would split a case of beer in the lunch room and head home. I simply headed home.

Another week passed and each morning on my way to the sweat shop I would deliberately drive past Lakeview generating station, and every morning I would see the picketers. But, on this second Friday of the strike, there were no picketers and I thought "what's going on?" Within seconds of this thought, the news came on the radio with the announcement that the Ontario Hydro strike was over. Halleluiah!

I continued on to the sweat shop however, and actually began working until the reality of it all hit me. What was I doing? The strike was over! So I went to the Managers office and explained my situation, and that I was done working there. He said he didn't want to lose me, that I was such a good worker and that he would match my Hydro salary. I thought "yea right!" He had no idea of what I did for hydro or how much I made, so I simply thanked him and was on my way. I went straight home, picked up Barb and headed for the beer store. I bought a case of beer and delivered it to the sweat shop lunch room, leaving a note saying 'Enjoy and Farewell.' Barb and I then went for lunch to celebrate, and then afterword, we bought Gary and Vicki new bikes. Why not, I was back in the money now. I got a call later that afternoon from hydro; officially informing me that the strike was over and to report to work on the following Tuesday as Monday was a statutory holiday and I would be paid for it. After hanging up, I said to Barb "What a wonderful company to work for."

CHAPTER 10

Career Change

IT WAS GREAT being back at the training centre again, and I was determined that I would never go on strike again. I was going to do everything in my power to get into management and it wasn't long after this thought, or I should say goal, that an Assistant Training Officer position was posted. I immediately applied, but so did many others. The competition was going to be tough. I started to prepare myself by researching training methodologies that were in vogue at the time. There was one in particular; called Criterion Referenced Instruction (CRI) that senior management seemed to be embracing at the time. This became my primary focus. Along with coming up to speed with the many technical aspects associated with training, I had to focus on my personal development as well, especially by making adjustments to the 'Lovable' aspect of my persona. This would be the hard part.

The interview was intense and conducted by two superintendents, two training officers and a human resource officer. Prior to the interview, each candidate was given a project based on CRI in which we had to make a presentation. Like most, I'm sure, I walked out of the interview not really knowing or sensing how I my performance was received. The selection process was a long one and it would be a number of weeks before the result would be announced. Work resumed as normal but there wasn't a day that went by that I didn't think about the interview, the competition and my strengths and weaknesses. Every day, someone anonymously, posted a sheet on the bulletin board that was written in racetrack form listing all the candidates and their order in the race, with each day the standings changing. I was usually in first, second or third place. It was cleverly done actually. I personally believe it was done by a woman in pay roll, and in the end the standings turned out to be somewhat accurate.

One day, not knowing it was judgement day; I noticed one of the candidates walking down the hall and heard him being called into the manager's office. That's it, I thought, he's got the job, game over. It was about eleven o'clock and my superintendent, Frank Butler came to my desk and asked me to follow him to his office. We entered and he told me to shut the door. After doing so, he reached out his hand to shake mine and said "Congratulations you got the job"

Frank added that there were two successful candidates. One of whom I didn't even know had applied. Her name was Judy O'Donnell, the manager's secretary. Frank told me to keep it all a secret until after lunch, when the other candidates were informed. I went back to my desk and phoned Barb at her work and whispered, ***"I got the job."*** I was so pumped up that I couldn't just sit at my desk and keep quiet, so I quietly snuck out of the office and went home for lunch.

Like all of the other candidates, I thought that the main criterion for the job was to have a strong technical/ training background. We didn't know or see the big picture. The department was expanding into areas beyond technical training and Judy fit the bill to a tee. She possessed strong communication, supervisory and other management skills which the training department needed. Not having this knowledge of the departments' foresight, a few of the unsuccessful candidates were vocally upset that Judy got the job, and one in particular was outraged. These negative feelings created a difficult environment for Judy, but it didn't take her long to prove that the right selection was made.

As for myself, I was pleased to receive sincere congratulations from most everyone. This meant a lot to me as I'm sure it would have to Judy as well. Later that afternoon, I was called into our manager's office for a little chat about my future, and all the new opportunities that lay in front of me. I was then informed of my new assignment. I would temporarily be reporting to Superintendent Dick Frampton, and under his direction, develop a new, two year Graduate Engineer Training Program based upon the methodology of Criterion Referenced Instruction. I had six weeks to complete the program upon which time, and under the auspices of Superintendent Frank Butler, I would introduce the training program to newly hired engineers, and monitor its effectiveness as well as the training performance of the grads. I would be the new, Graduate Engineer, Training Officer. I was swollen with pride to the point of bursting, and was about to experience one of the most exciting, challenging and happiest times of my life. Thanks again mom and dad, I know you've been instrumental in opening this door for me.

I tackled this new project with lust, utter lust. As I have said, I am not one for lunch breaks or coffee breaks, so I literally locked myself in a spare room and toiled away. In developing this training program, I didn't reinvent the wheel. I used as much as possible, existing and proven material from various programs that I researched, and then basically cut and pasted the objectives and criterion, for clerical to process and put together in the proper format. When the program was complete, Dick Frampton arranged for me to give a presentation to a group of supervisors, engineers and the assistant manager at the Lakeview Generating Station for the purpose of critiquing, and providing us with feedback. The CRI methodology was new to these people and not something they were familiar with, so it was initially, negatively received. I strongly believed in this program, but I could also understand their hang ups. So, I put on my salesman's hat and went to work tackling their negatives. In the end, I felt that the majority of the audience felt more comfortable with what the training program could achieve, compared to their *old school* methods. When I returned to the office later that day, Dick Frampton had already received the feedback. It wasn't all positive, but it was good enough to to get the go ahead. One negative comment was from the assistant manager who thought that I came across too defensive. Well of course I did! I was defending what I believed in.

My next step was to develop a one week indoctrination program for the new grads which would introduce them to their new employer, Ontario Hydro, Thermal Generation and all things pertinent to them, especially the requirements of their two year training program. I was informed that their start date would be the first week in December. I also had to arrange hotel accommodations and set up a little meet, greet and welcoming party. I arranged a large suite at their hotel to be used for the meet and greet and it would also serve as accommodation for me. I planned to bring in some beer, wine and sandwiches for the occasion, but before doing so, I received a call from Human Resources at head office asking what my plans were. They didn't like the idea of my picnic. They told me that I was going to host and welcome gradate engineers into the organization and they weren't going to be nickel and dimed. I was told to set up hotel catering for the occasion. I was quickly learning that there was a difference between management hires and union hires, and trying to be frugal wasn't going to cut it. I did as I was told.

The meet and greet was held on a Sunday night and went smoothly. I very much enjoyed talking and getting to know each and every one of these grads, and felt very comfortable with them individually and as a group. I am also sure that my picnic would have suited them just fine. I can't even remember what was catered.

The one week indoctrination session started the next morning. I had scheduled a number of guest speakers to make presentations on things that would be directly important to the grads, everything from payroll to health and safety. My boss, Superintendent Frank Butler, kicked off the session by giving an overview of the organizations hierarchy and where we all fit in. Following this, I gave a presentation on their training program and performance expectations. I explained that each one of them, after reporting to their respective stations, would begin their training rotations in Operations for a period of three months. They would be assigned to a crew, work shift work and learn in detail the operation of a Thermal Generating Station. I explained that although they were management personnel they would get a lot more out of their training if they took off their iron rings, and become a part of the crew, or one of the boys so to say. I suggested that they get involved socially even in off shift activities. Doing so would go a long way in their being treated as an equal, and they would likely be allowed to get some hands on operating experience that they would otherwise not be allowed. One grad in particular took this to heart. He removed his ring and never wore it at work for the twenty five years that I had association with him. He was also known as the most down to earth and likable engineers in the organization. This came as no surprise to me, because after his graduated from university, jobs were scarce so he flipped burgers at Mc Donald's. That to me was true grit.

Near the end of the indoctrination, I received word that the stations didn't want the grads to report until January of the New Year, because of budgetary constraints. For the next two weeks the grads, unexpectedly, became my responsibility. My only guide line was to keep them busy and entertain them. Entertain them I did. The first order of business was transportation so I rented a mini bus. Every morning I would pick them up at their hotel and take them on tours to places like the Niagara Falls, Sir Adam Beck Hydroelectric Station or the Lakeview Thermal Generating Station in Mississauga and of course, System Control, the hub and brains behind power distribution throughout the province.

One morning, I arranged a meeting at Head Office with Joe Walters the Director, and soon to be appointed Vise-President of the Thermal and Hydroelectric Division. The only down side to this meeting was me driving a mini bus in downtown Toronto and having to parallel parking it. Hiding my nervousness, I aced it perfectly like it's something I did every day. The grads were impressed and applauded me. The meeting was set for 10 am in the board room, and at 1010, Joe showed up all apologetic for being late as he was dealing with a potential crisis of low lake levels, hindering power production at the hydroelectric stations. I couldn't believe it, here was the director making apologies for being late for something as insignificant as a meet and greet, compared to a crisis in the provinces electrical power supply. This was the first time that I had met Joe, but during his presentation he often made reference to me, as though he had known me for years. I was proud and in awe. I was to have association with Joe many times in the future, but the most memorable get together, was in a washroom at a grad conference dinner in a hotel in downtown Toronto. Joe was a smoker as I was at the time. We were the only smokers at the conference, so after dinner we met in the washroom for a puff. We talked about our dependence on cigarettes, and because Hydro had a no smoking policy in the workplace, Joe said that he was thinking of quitting. I thought he meant quit smoking, and was totally shocked to learn that he meant quitting "Ontario Hydro."

The New Year came and the grads reported to their prospective stations, and I, for the next two years monitored their training program and performance. The hiring of grads was an ongoing process and as the numbers increased, so did my responsibilities and travel. After a few years in this position it was time to move on to bigger and better things.

Promotion

DURING MY CAREER with Ontario Hydro, I can honestly say, that there was never a boring or monotonous period of work activity. Take for example a looming strike by the Power Workers Union. It was imminent, and management was gearing up for it by training its personnel to perform certain jobs in order to keep some of the power plants running. Having an electrical background I was certain that I would work in that capacity, however, the powers that be, assigned me to be a heavy equipment operator in the coal yard at the Nanticoke G.S. on Lake Erie. Go figure? There were three of us from the training department assigned to a crew that would travel to Detroit Michigan for training on bull dozers, and earth moving equipment. This would be a covert operation, to be performed at night. The reason being, should the union of that organization (which I won't mention by name) who would be training us, learn who we were and why we were being trained, they would have shut us down. The first phase of our training was theoretical, air breaks, safety, and an intro to the machines we would be driving. The second phase was driving or should I say, trying to drive the machines. The first vehicle was a D9 Bulldozer. Driving a bulldozer at night and on a black coal field was one heck of an experience, and I don't know why they were equipped with head lights, because they didn't light up anything. The main objective was to push coal forward while keeping the blade completely horizontal. Sounds easy, but it's not. On my fist attempt at driving the dozer, I thought that I was keeping the blade horizontal, but I soon learned that I was not; it was more like keeping the blade vertical as I drove the dozer towards the centre of the earth. When I got off the D9, the crew were in hysterics. They nick named me "Dive Dive" as though I was a submarine operator. I did sort of get the hang of it though, enough to graduate to the monster earth moving machine. After our week of training it was time to return home and get ready to transfer to Nanticoke G.S. The very next morning we learned that Hydro and the union reached a deal, and a strike was averted.

Soon after my heavy equipment training, there was a change in the management hierarchy, and I received a promotion as a result. I also assumed a new work assignment. For the next few months I would carry out a Needs Analysis of Ontario Hydro's supply division. The objective was to determine ways of reducing inefficiencies etc; in order to save at least a million dollars per annum in supply costs. I was chosen for this assignment because of my training in this methodology. I would be required to travel throughout the province and interview staff at all hydro locations, Nuclear, Thermal and Hydroelectric, as well as inspect work environments, examine procedures, and make observations of work practices.

CHAPTER 11

Vicki Summers

AT ABOUT THE same time as I was to start my needs analysis, my daughter Vicki finished her first year of college and was looking for a summer job. I took her resume to our Senior Clerk Liz Knight, and asked if she could forward it to other hydro departments in the area, emphasizing "other departments." About a week later Liz approached me and said that she was going to interview Vicki for a summer job at TTD. I said no way. I didn't want her working in the same office. I didn't believe in nepotism. By the way I asked, "What would be the pay for a summer student?" Liz said "about $500.00 a week" and I said, "Wow! Go ahead and interview her." Vicki got the job as a word processor, and other duties as required. It worked out well, she did a good job, was well liked, and I hardly had association with her at the office, as I was travelling most of the summer. There was no 'daddy' interference. A week prior to her start date, and before I hit the road, I took Vicki to L.A. Barb couldn't go because of her work at the Licence Office. We toured Hollywood, Universal Studios and then we drove down to San Diego to tour the U.S. Naval base where I took my Basic Training, followed by Electricians Mate 'A' school. It was a wonderful trip, and we returned fresh and ready to go. I must mention that prior to that summer; we had extensive renovations done to our house on Canterbury Rd. During the process, the contractor's son took a shine to Vicki. Old fashioned as he was the contractor asked me if his son could ask Vicki out on a date. His name was Mike, and I was impressed with him, so I agreed. They would marry a couple of years later. The summer flew by; I completed my needs analysis and presented the results to the powers that be. Although some of my recommendations were accepted, they were not immediately implemented, and I learned much later on, that some of the key recommendations were acted upon, but the credit to their success was given to others. Alas.

Our Beautiful Daughter
Victoria Lee Summers

Quitting a Forty Year Habit

AROUND THE EARLY nineties, cigarette smoking became increasingly socially unacceptable. Although I would make myself scarce and sneak a smoke here and there, it wouldn't go unnoticed because of the lingering smell on my cloths. Then one morning, as I stepped out of my office into the hallway, I heard a voice say; "Hey Gary it works!" It was Bob from a neighboring office, and I said; "What works?" He said the patch, the Nicoderm patch. I'd never heard of it, but after he explained how it worked, and that he wasn't experiencing withdrawal, I immediately made a doctor's appointment for a prescription. (Required at that time) I had tried to quit a few times, but I became too miserable, especially with my family, but I was motivated to succeed this time. It was a Tuesday at 1:40 pm; I put out the last cigarette from my pack and put on a Nicoderm, Step 1 patch. Because of my past behaviour when quitting, my wife Barb (a smoker herself) was sceptical about this process, and didn't bring attention to it until the second day. She said; "I have to ask, how you are feeling?"

I said, "I feel great! and I'm not experiencing any withdraw." So about a week later, Barb went on the patch. I must say that the patch worked on me better, and was easier than Barbs experience, but succeed we did. We made a pact that we would open a separate bank account, even at a separate bank from ours, and deposit the money that we would have spent on cigarettes, every Friday after work. At the time it was costing, between us, a $100.00 a week. About a year later we had saved $5500.00 and celebrated being smoke free, by taking a two week trip to England to visit Barbs family and tour the country, doing bed and breakfasts. Much better than $5500.00 going up in smoke.

CHAPTER 12

Farewell Ontario Hydro

Sudden Retirement

IT WAS THE month of March when Barb and I returned from England, and I looked forward to getting back to work, Barb not so much though. Back at the office, the talk of the day was the financial crisis that Ontario Hydro was facing, and there were tons of rumors as to what was going to happen. There were rumors of layoffs, buyouts, early retirement incentives, and the closing down of departments that provide non essential services. It was a situation that long term employees would never have dreamed of happening, but happening it was. Soon an announcement was made that the Chairman of Ontario Hydro would address all employees via a live media broadcast the following week. During that period of time, waiting for the chairman's address, and amid everyone's speculation and personal fears as to how bad the situation was, I would guess that work production in the company was at an all-time low. Finally the day came, and while employees were glued to their monitors, the chairman started off by describing the big picture, and explaining the need to downsize. He also explained that there were generous options available to all employees, which was based on years of service and seniority. My option was to take the early retirement incentive, or continue working under a cloud of uncertainty.

The early retirement package was very lucrative. It was offered to employees that had at least 25 years of service, of which I had just achieved a few weeks prior. It came with a hefty lump sum cash payout, a no age penalty pension that was indexed to the cost of living for life, health benefits, life insurance and an unused vacation buy back. I was only 48 years old at the time and wasn't ready to retire, but more than that, I loved my job. To continue working for hydro with an uncertain future, however, was not an option so I decided to retire. The retirement date was dictated by hydro. It had to be no later than November 1st of that year. In the end, Ontario Hydro downsized, from approximately 27,000 employees to approximately 17,000 employees, and the lights still stayed on. Amazing!

I might add that prior to this unsettling news; we had sold our home on Canterbury Rd, and moved outside of Mississauga to the village of Clarkson, where we were renting an executive town house. It had all the amenities, tennis, squash, racquet ball, swimming pool and a social club. Perfect for retirement, but a bit too pricey so we decided to move to a lower cost of living area, and buy a house.

We decided on Niagara Falls. It was a border town that offered interesting travel opportunities, and the price of homes were half that of Mississauga. The first house that we viewed had what we were looking for, plus a swimming pool, so we made an offer, and it was accepted. The closing date was October 1st so I would have to retire a month earlier than planned. Our daughter Vicki was now working for HEPCO, a credit union serving the financial needs of hydro employees. She had been living at home with us, but now it was time to leave the nest. It was a difficult time because; Vicki wasn't living at home like a daughter, but living in our home as a friend. She found a nice basement apartment by the lake and close to her work. Prior to our move to Niagara, Vicki moved into her apartment. It was surreal what was happening in our lives; even going to work for the final weeks was strange, because there were no immediate, or future goals, or targets for the training department, productivity was almost nonexistent. As I had achieved my 25 years of service, I was to be awarded a gold watch. I was given a brochure that contained several choices. I chose a ladies watch. It displayed the hydro logo (The Plug) with a small diamond representing 12 o'clock. When asked why I chose a ladies watch, I replied, that it was for my wife, because if it wasn't for her, and making me less lovable, I'd probably not have made it to 25 years. She still has the watch, a wears it every day.

CHAPTER 13

Niagara Falls

MY DAY OF retirement came, and in the early afternoon, I quietly disappeared from the office. I lacked the courage to go around and say good bye to everyone because I would be an emotional mess. So I just went home. It was strange getting up the next morning and not going to work. It was eerie. Barb still had a couple of weeks before she would retire, so I spent my time boxing up odds and ends and taking them to a storage facility in Niagara to lessen the moving day load. On the morning before the closing date of our house, I began suffering severe abdominal pains. I had never experienced such pain. Finally after fighting it and going through denial, Barb called an ambulance and off to Emergency I went.

I don't remember a lot of what was going on other than I just wanted to die, but I do remember the surgeon over the intercom saying; "I want Summers brought to surgery yesterday." It turned out that it was the chief surgeon who operated on me and saved my life. My bowel had ruptured and I was in critical condition and really not expected to live. Barb was asked if she wanted to have last rights administered. Poor Barb, after four hours of surgery and me lying there in intensive care with tubes, wires and whatever else was protruding from me, she had to deal with the house closing, moving, and a host of other things. She made one phone call. The call was to my best friend Rick Crown and Barb simply said HELP!

Rick was also taking the early retirement package but was still working at the training centre until November 1st. He quickly organized a work party to take care of all the moving requirements. People from all levels at the training centre got involved and took care of everything, relieving Barb of a ton of weight from her shoulders, and the mental anxiety and stress that she was suffering. I was in intensive care for two weeks and was not completely out of danger for a number of days. At one point, even our lawyer travelled from Niagara to have me (when I was able) sign some real-estate documents. Everything miraculously came together all at once. Thanks mom and dad, and of course my friends at TTD.

Although I had a colostomy and had to wear a bag, I rebounded rather quickly. The day before being released from the hospital, I walked down the hall to the nurses' station where the chief surgeon happened to be. He looked at me and shook his head with a smile. He said that it was hard to believe that I was actually alive and walking. After what I had been through, I didn't fully realise how bad my situation was. He clarified it by saying that I was only minutes from death. Upon him saying that I simply broke down and cried.

He then told me that the colostomy could be reversed, but I would have to wait at least six months for the surgery. I then asked him if I would be able to drive home to Niagara the next day and he said; "if you could drive before you came in, then yes you can drive home."

The next morning Vicki brought my car to the hospital, and after dropping her off at her apartment, I headed for Niagara. Barb warmly greeted me at the door but looked stressed out as well. She should have been after all she went through. The house was in disarray with boxes unpacked, furniture to be moved and a lot of cleaning to be done. We quickly got to it and before long we were settled in. The first order of business was to realize some of our retirement plans. We purchased identical bikes and of course would have to wait till spring to go touring, but until then we bought cross country skis to occupy our winter leisure. There was plenty to do to keep us busy like redecorating the house, which started with gutting the kitchen and redoing the cupboards, from dark walnut to white melamine. As well we explored areas in Niagara that we didn't realize existed. On one of our outings I asked a man what winter was like in Niagara and he said; "It would snow at times but be melted by noon" Yea right! It started snowing on Halloween and never stopped until April.

I've never shovelled so much in my entire life. On the social side, we started going to a pub called Hogan's. We met a couple there that had also retired from hydro and moved to Niagara, they lived just a few blocks from us. We became friends and did some exploring together. We also got to know the owners of the pub, Carman and Valarie Baralaro. In fact, in time, we became good friends. There were always snide remarks and jokes that we often heard around the area that Carman was connected to the mafia but we shrugged it off as hearsay.

The NFL Super Bowl was coming up and it was Dallas against Buffalo. Carman casually said; "Gary, I'll bet you straight up that Dallas wins. I'll bet one thousand dollars to your one dollar with a limit of ten." I wasn't great at math, but it was pretty easy to figure that the most I could lose would be ten dollars, and yet I could win ten thousand dollars. I jumped right on that bet and started to said to a guy next to me to get in on it, but Carman interrupted and pointed out that it was only one wager, and only with me. On super bowl night, Barb and I reserved a table by the big screen TV. When Carman came in I said; "Got the cash?" and he quickly displayed a roll of cash like I had never seen before. Needless to say, I paid Carman my ten dollars at the end of the night. Oh well it was exciting and Carman and I were to do a lot of wagering in the future. Not big wagers but more for bragging rights. He once said to Barb; "I do some high stake betting but I get more enjoyment betting Gary that all the others. More about Carman later.

My six months of being on a colostomy bag came to an end in March. I went back to Mississauga for the successful reversal. It seemed strange to me though, that the morning of the surgery I was super nervous. It was as though I had gotten so used to the bag that I could have carried on the rest of my life with it. By the way, during the six month period of my colostomy, I did volunteer work at the Niagara General Hospital. I volunteered with the intent of offering support and advice to anyone that would have to go through the procedure, however, because of my training and technical background, the nurse in charge of volunteers had other plans for me. I was basically working in her office and in time I felt I was doing most of her work. That was not what I had volunteered for, so after a time, I withdrew my services.

Summer time came and out came the bikes. I bought a bike rack and we would head for the Niagara Parkway. Almost every day, we would bike for an hour or so, then BBQ and read our books by the river. There is only so much biking and picnicking that one can do without getting bored and I was getting bored.

I was always energetic and had to keep moving, so I decided to look for a job. It didn't matter what type of job, just a job to keep me bus, so I checked out the want ads. I came across an ad for a customer service, shuttle driver at a local car dealership. I went directly to the dealership with my resume and applied. The son of the owner interviewed me and felt that I was over qualified. I explained that I was the type of person who just needed to work. Money wasn't an issue. I just needed to work. He hired me and I started the next day. It was a full time job and after a while Barb started wondering why I retired if I'm back to working full time. After a while I agreed with her and decided to compromise my need to work by finding something part time, two or three days a week would be ideal. Sort of semi retirement. I quit the dealership and applied for a part time job through Manpower. My first job was at an electrical supply company in Welland, three days a week. After a while I was asked to work full time making deliveries. I did this for a while until I found myself in the same situation as before, not retired. I went back to Manpower and was assigned all sorts of part time jobs from working in green houses to demolition. One day I got a call to report to a company called ECHO. It was a three day stint, doing inventory of their baking and kitchen products. I guess they like my work because the following week they called Manpower and requested my services in shipping and receiving. After a couple of weeks the manager asked if I would work for them permanently three days a week. I accepted and was trained on various warehouse machines and became a shipper/receiver.

One cold and bleak February morning, and out of the blue I got a call from a company called Royal Steward and Associates. The owner and General Manager, Tom Robinson, who also took early retirement from Hydro, asked if I would be interested in doing a Safety Audit for an electrical utility in St. Lucia. Tom had said that I came highly recommended. (I'd like to note that before I retired from hydro and along with my other responsibilities; I was the Team Leader of Occupational skills overseeing a team of instructors in charge of Health and Safety, First Aid, Driver Training, Work Protection Code etc.) After Tom explained the details, professional fee, per diem, accommodations and travel, I jumped at the opportunity. (About ten feet in the air) The audit was to be carried out in March.

CHAPTER 14

St Lucia

THE CARIBBEAN IN March. I couldn't believe my good fortune. Tom told me that my fee wasn't a king's ransom, but yes it was Tom, It was huge by my standards. I think I would have conducted the audit for expenses only. I met with Tom shortly after and was briefed on what to expect and to discuss their terms of reference. All travel arrangements were made for me and soon I was off the Jewel of the Caribbean. The plane landed in the south of the island near a city called Vieux Fort. Transportation was waiting for me and we drove for about an hour north to the capital city of Castries. From there we headed up a mountain to my hotel called The Green Parrot. Although it was quite satisfactory, it had seen better days. It was quite popular at one time, even hosting England's Prince Charles. It was Saturday when I arrived so I had the rest of the weekend to explore the surrounding area. The hotel was somewhat isolated, so on Sunday I took a taxi to the city of Castries. Sunday is not the day to discover the city as everything, and I mean everything, is closed. I headed back to the hotel and spent the rest of the day beside the pool. The following morning my driver showed up to take me to the head office of Lucelec the Islands electrical utility. My driver was the companies Training Officer and would be my main contact during my stay.

The first order of business was to meet with all of the department managers to explain what I would be examining during the audit, and collect from them their areas of concern. They voiced no areas of concern but there should have been. I was assigned a young engineer to chauffer me throughout the island, visiting all of the utilities work sites. I examined and interviewed employees' from all branches, Administration, Generation and Transmission and Distribution. It didn't take long to learn that Health and

Safety was not part of the makeup of Lucelec. Basic safety equipment such as hard hats, safety glasses, work boots, hearing protection was foreign to these people. I watched workers with pick axes hacking at the ground wearing nothing but open toed sandals. Workers were working aloft with no fall protection. Compared to the industrial standards in North America and Europe this was a horror story. At the end of the week I gave a verbal exit report of my findings to the managers and submitted my written audit report a week later.

The report was scathing and was directed at senior management for their total lack of concern for health and safety in the work place. Working conditions were primitive to say the least. When the Managing Director read the report he went ballistic and came down hard on his management team. Things were going to change and I was going to be a part of that change.

A few months after my assignment at Lucelec, I was requested back to carry out a separate audit concentrating solely on the Transmission and Distribution Department. I could see some small but positive changes starting to take place at the utility. The M. D. was taking my report and recommendations very seriously. In fact over the ensuing years all of my recommendations (with the exception of one) had been implemented. Besides conducting annual H&S audits at Lucelec, I performed other work as well, such as; developing on-the-job training for operators. I ran several supervisor training workshops as well, and during the final year of my involvement with Lucelec, they achieved what a few years earlier I would have thought impossible, 'No lost time accidents for an entire year.' On my last visit to St. Lucia, I was honored with a farewell dinner and presented with a gold watch and a plaque thanking me for my involvement. That evening employees showed up at my hotel to say goodbye and presented me with personal gifts. My eyes flooded.

Being an associate of Royal Steward, I was offered various consulting assignments that were always interesting and yet challenging. After a few years in the business, Tom Robinson, the General Manager, decided to retire the company. I had already formed my own company called Q2A (Questions to Answers) and was now on my own. I never advertised myself and never really needed to, because phone calls and emails came out of the blue requesting my services. These requests stemmed from word-of-mouth, recommendations. My wife Barb also benefitted from these assignments as she would accompany me on some of my trips. There was always variety for me, whether it was Gas Turbine training in Newfoundland, Needs Analysis in Washington State, Accident Investigation workshops in the Cayman Islands, or technical training somewhere in the Caribbean.

Dominica

THERE WAS ONE particular trip however; that I was glad Barb didn't accompany me. I was asked by Carelec (an organization that provided training resources for a host of Caribbean nations) to co-chair a Health and Safety Conference on the island of Dominica. It was in February, and the day before and the morning of, my departure, we got hit with a bad snow storm. I stayed in a hotel near the Buffalo Airport the night before, and arrived at the airport early the next morning, but the plane was delayed, and didn't take off for hours. Our schedule was to land in New Jersey; change planes there, and head for Antigua, for yet another plane change to Dominica. Because of our late arrival in New Jersey, we missed our connecting flight to Antigua, so the airlines put us up in a hotel until the next morning. On top of that, they lost my luggage. Early the next morning, I went to the airport and thankfully found my luggage. When we arrived in Antigua, I was told that my flight to Dominica was booked for the previous day and because of that, they couldn't accommodate me, as the next flight was full. Talk about stress! In the mean time, a Carelec Representative had called my home wondering where I was. Barb simply told him, that I was trying to get there. Finally after wrangling, begging and pleading, I managed to fly to Dominica. The bus ride to the hotel was disgustingly uncomfortable. Two people had to get off the bus to be sick during the hour and a half ride. Finally I made it; only 24 hours late and with thirty five people waiting for me, I was not happy. Early the next morning as I headed for the shower I broke my toe on a French provincial, protruding table leg. I was not happy. As co chair of the Health and Safety Conference, I limped embarrassingly to my place on the dais. I was in pain, and I was not happy.

The morning after the end of the conference, I headed home, or should I say, I tried to. I managed the uncomfortable hour and a half ride to the Dominica airport and arrived in Antigua on time, however, once there, we sat for ages wondering why we weren't boarding, it turned out that the airplane had a flat tire and it had to be changed. Needless to say we arrived late in New Jersey and I had to scramble to catch the last flight to Buffalo, broken toe and all. Oh the pain, trying to run with a broken and swelled toe. I just made it to the gate as they were closing the hatch, but then, I had to face a chorus of boos from my fellow passengers disgruntled about my causing their delay. I was not happy.

We finally arrived in Buffalo, but of course, characteristic to the whole trip, my luggage didn't. On top of that, and because of a security warning sign about keys, before I flew out of Buffalo, my car keys were in my checked luggage. Disheartened I took the shuttle bus to my hotel. I was frustrated and tired, but I couldn't sleep, I just wanted to go home, so at 2 am I called AAA to come and make a key for my car. Crossing the border was another issue, because of being away a week and not having anything to declare, not even luggage. I finally made it home and woke Barb to get in the house. That afternoon I got a call from the airport saying they found my luggage and would deliver it between 10 pm and midnight. I explained to them that there would be no way I'd be up at that time; I was totally exhausted, so I asked that the luggage be delivered the next day. When I got up the next morning, low and behold, there was my luggage, sitting right in the middle of the driveway, which had probably been there for hours, just ripe for being stolen. I won't get into the details, and follow up frustrations with the airline as I tried to get compensation for the cost of a locksmith, and compensation for all my troubles. They said that I would get a discount on my next flight with them. I said; "there would never, ever, be a next flight with them." And there wasn't.

CHAPTER 15

Technical Training Once Again

OUT OF THE blue I got a call from a training group based in Saskatchewan asking if I would be interested in working with them, in which I replied I would. The first course would be Electrical Troubleshooting; I would sit-in with one of their instructors for a week and then take over the next class. So off to Vancouver I went. It was one of those discount flights that landed in every city across Canada and it seemed like forever before I got there. The sit-in went well however, and I agreed to deliver the next course in Regina. After the Regina course, I sat in on another, more advanced Electrical course at a mine in Logan British Columbia; where similarly, I took over the next scheduled course. Then things got a little iffy when I cashed a pay check and it bounced. The head of the training group assured me that he would make it right and after a while he did, kind of. The next course I was to be involved with was scheduled to be delivered at the Canought Hotel in Hamilton. The hotel had seen better days, but at one time, it had been very prominent and popular. I checked in the night before and was to meet with a co-instructor the following day. When I went to the training room to prepare, I was shocked to find our shipped equipment in total disarray. A big part of the course content was computer based, but there were no computers. They were stolen. When my co-instructor showed up, I found out that this was the second time it had happened, and at the same hotel. We called the police and informed management staff. Although there were strong suspicions as to who did it, there was no proof. My experienced, co-instructor said that he could salvage most of the course in some way or another, but I had had enough and bid farewell to that organization for more than one reason. I was pleased to learn that shortly after this episode; the hotel was shut down, with plans to restore it to its former extravagance. I hope that the computer thief made enough money from his bounty to support himself forever after losing his job, and I'm sure that with the strong suspicion that surrounded him, he didn't get rehired when the new hotel opened.

Then one day, shortly after, I got another call out of the blue, asking me if I'd be interested in doing some electrical training at the Pickering Nuclear Station on Lake Ontario.

The call came from a consulting company that was commissioned to provide technical services and training for Ontario Hydro's Pickering Nuclear Station. I never did find out how or where they found out about me but I was honoured. The contract would be for three months, and although it was the most lucrative offer I've ever had, this request wouldn't be that easy to accept. It would require me to be away from home and living in a hotel five nights a week. After a couple of weeks of deep pondering and lengthy discussions with Barb, we decided to accept. When the Manager of the Pickering Nuclear Training Centre called me, however, he explained that it was instrumentation training that they wanted me for and not electrical. I explained to him that I had some instrumentation training years before but it was not my forte. He asked me if I could handle the basics and gave me some examples of what I would be required to deliver. I felt confident enough and agreed to do it.

Pickering, Station 'A' had been shut down some year's prior, but was now going through an extensive rehab in order to be put back in service. As a result there was a hiring frenzy going on. These new hires required training, and that's where I came in.

I showed up at the Pickering Training Centre two weeks before Christmas. The plan was for me to sit-in on instrument training session number one, and then after the New Year, deliver the following sessions on my own. After my two weeks of 'sitting in' and some home study during the holidays, I felt confident that I could do a good job. More than feeling confident, I felt reborn. I felt I was back in the groove again, back to contributing and making a positive change in human performance. Empowering people with the skills and knowledge required to do their job. It felt like a miracle to be back and it was. Thanks mom and dad. I was also pleased and surprised to see so many familiar faces sitting in my classes. The coal fired, Lakeview G.S. had shut down, and as a result, many of the technical trades had transferred to nuclear. It turned out that I had trained some of these technicians some years ago when they were electrical apprentices. It certainly was like old times again

A couple of months later, I was asked if I would extend my contract and deliver the session two courses. I've always had trouble saying no so I continued on. In fact, my initial three month contract turned out to be three years. I somehow managed through self training and tutoring from colleagues, to be a competent instructor in all areas of Instrumentation. I was proud of that accomplishment. In the end however, I was so sick of hotels and restaurants, that I still have problems with them. It wasn't just while I was living out of town; it was also when I came home on weekends because Barb and I always ate out. During that time however, the money was good, and I was able to buy a motorcycle and a twenty eight foot cabin cruiser. We belonged to a boat club for a few years and really enjoyed it. It was a weekend haven, almost like living in cottage country.

Gary Summers Jr.

WHILE WRITING THIS memoir I seldom mentioned our son Gary for the simple reason that we basically disowned him. As a young teenager Gary was a good lad. He had good work ethics and proved very responsible, whether it was delivering newspapers or working as a stock boy for a local grocery store. We trusted him and even bought him a new car which was to be shared between him and his mom. Only a few days after getting the car I noticed traces of cigarette ashes adhered to the driver's side of the car. I took a closer look and saw a large cigarette burn on the front seat. I couldn't believe what I saw. When confronting him about it, he said he didn't know anything about it, and denied the obvious, over and over. To make a long story short, Gary got into the wrong crowd and lied about many things, and did a lot of sneaky things, like stealing liquor from the liquor cabinet, drinking it, and then topping the bottle up with water. He snuck beer into his room at night, and hid the bottles in the attic. Things were going downhill fast. As far as I was concerned there was only one answer and that was for him to join the military, and let them straighten him out. I took him to the naval recruiting office but he didn't have the qualifications for them but he did for the army. Off to basic training he went and after completing it, I started to regain some pride in him. From there he went to Cyprus as a U.N. Peace Keeper. Things were looking up but not for long. After Cyprus he was transferred to the Princess Ann Paratroopers out west. At that point, life started to fall apart for Gary. Drinking and drugs, and who knows what else. One night he was so high, he tried to parachute off a building but he didn't have a parachute, and broke most of the bones in his body. That was it for the army, they dishonorably discharged him, and that was it for us. We disowned him. Gary became a homeless person living on the streets of Victoria BC. We had no contact with him. One day a few years later our daughter Vicki called to tell us that Gary had found where she lived and wanted to talk to her, and that he hadn't had a drink or drug in a year, he belonged to AA and was clean. She agreed to see him. She said that he had changed and was very remorseful about his past and wanted to talk to Barb and myself. Reluctantly we agreed and met him at Vicki's house. It was tense but Gary felt proud that he achieved a full year of being sober, and that there was a special AA meeting planned to celebrate the occasion. Gary had a job driving a truck, he owned a car, and had a supportive girl friend and things were looking up.

Gary lived with his dog, in a basement apartment in Hamilton. We took him out for lunch one day and after, we met his girl friend at her work. He showed us his apartment and as it was lacking a few pieces of furniture we told him we would supply it. I was still working at Pickering and would drop off the furniture the following weekend. We also celebrated that Christmas at our house in Niagara.

Then we got a call one day from Vicki, saying that Gary was in the hospital. It had something to do with codeine that he had taken for a tooth ache. I didn't fully understand it, but I left Pickering and visited him at the hospital. He said that he was hard up for money, and that his car was towed, and impounded for an overnight parking violation. I used an ATM at the hospital and gave him five hundred dollars. He was then discharged, got his car out of impoundment, and that was the last time I would see Gary. His girl friend had spent a day trying to contact him but couldn't, so she called the police. The police broke into his apartment and found him dead, sitting in front of the TV with his dog going wild at the police. After an autopsy was conducted, the coroner called me and explained they could not find a cause for his death. There was neither alcohol nor drugs on the premises or in him. As far as the doctor was concerned, Gary just died. Thirty years old, in good shape from weight training and he just died.

We arranged his funeral and had him cremated and buried at the Fairview cemetery in Niagara Falls.

Gary Summers Jr.

Carmen Baralaro

I PREVIOUSLY MENTIONED that Carmen Baralaro was the owner of Hogans Road House, our local pub, and had become good friends. We had a lot of associations from Bocce Ball tournaments, wagering on sports, to social get-togethers. I also mentioned that there were rumors that Carmen was connected to the mafia. Well that turned out to be true, which had been unknown to us. Barb and I really liked Carmen, his wife Valerie and their two daughters. He was enjoyable to be around. One afternoon we were sitting around chatting and I brought up the subject of the Cedar Springs Racquet Club and my close association with owner Vic Mancini. I told Carmen stories of how I always beat Vic at chess, and how we attended a private party that was also attended by the notorious Johnny Papalia (Johnny Pops) and other stories that I thought he would find interesting, but Carmen just listened and never said a word. As we would find out later, Carmen was also a friend and associate of Vic Mancini and the two were Lieutenants under Papalia. When I was telling Carmen all those mafia stories and my innocent connections, he must have been thinking 'who the hell is this guy Gary?' 'How much does he know?' Well as it turned out, Johnny Pops was gunned down a short time later. It was a mafia hit and Carmen, still unknown to me at the time, took over the reins. One evening a few months later, Carmen's wife and children left their home to go shopping. Carmen was talking on the phone when there was a knock at the door. Not hanging up the phone Carmen answered the door and was facing a hit man. Carmen ran down the hall but changed his mind suddenly, turned and lunged at the gun man. Carmen was shot in the forehead, dead. It was heart breaking to see Valerie and her girls being filmed by the news after returning home to discover Carmen dead at the front door.

A few days later Barb and I attended Carmen's viewing at the funeral home, and his funeral which followed. I could not believe the strength displayed by Carmen's daughters as they delivered the eulogy. I have never seen anyone exhibit such strength, so soon after such a tragedy and yet being so young. Amen!

Royalty

SINCE MY SISTER and I were little tots, we heard quite often that we were from British Royalty; we were blue bloods but nothing further than that. No other details. A friend of my sister who was a professional ancestry researcher offered to trace our family's ancestry free of charge with emphasis on the Hilborn side. The following is the result of her research and in the end "The mysterious Mary, the Queens daughter" has been solved.

1. Henry VIII's sixth wife Katherine Parr, twice widowed and childless, wed Henry in 1543 but she was in love with Thomas Seymour, brother of Henrys 3rd wife Jane Seymour. Katherine remained faithful to Henry.

2. When Henry died, however, Katherine married in haste to Thomas. This created a lot of controversy. Katherine was 35 years old when she became pregnant in November, 1547. She gave birth to Mary Seymour on August 30, 1548.

Katherine died of sepsis (childbirth fever) September 5, 1548.

3. Mary was placed in the household of Thomas's brother the Duke of Summerset. There was political turmoil at the time and Mary was put in the care of the Duchess of Suffolk who resented the cost.

4. In 1550 Parliament restored Mary's title to her father's property. Stories circulated that Mary died young but the strongest theory of her whereabouts was that she was cared for by a northern family until she married a courtier (commoner)

5. Listed in the official records Mary (no last name given) married Thomas Hilborn in 1565. He was born in summerset England and from there, the ancestry paper- trail leads to my mother. Pauline Helen Hilborn.

Victorian writer Agnes Strictland's research indicates that the Seymours fell from grace and power. Mary's father Thomas was hanged and Edward was arrested in 1549 and jailed in the tower of London. People wanted the Seymour's to suffer. Mary was in a precarious position, and by not claiming her estate and disappearing, she would be safe and people would think she was dead.

Researcher Lynda Starbuck also wrote about Mary and called it a 'Royal Mystery'.

CHAPTER 16

To an Answer

WHEN WE MOVED to Niagara from Mississauga we knew nothing about the town or residential areas or what were good areas, what were bad areas or the in-between. Our affordability led us to an area in between. In the beginning it was acceptable enough, we had good neighbors but as time went on the good neighbors moved away and were replaced by a lower standard of people. A much lower standard. On one side lived a drug dealer. On the other side, a weirdo bitch. Across the street lived an old and low life Hag, whose daughter was a stripper and prostitute, her son was serving time in the big house. It was time to move. We enlisted a real-estate agent to sell our house and in the mean time, and quite by accident, I came across a house on Brookfield Ave that was listed for sale. I came to find out that Brookfield was considered an upscale neighborhood inhabited by mostly professional people, doctors, dentists, lawyers etc. I contacted our agent immediately to set up a viewing which he did. Within seconds of entering the house I was sold. It was custom built in the mid 50's by a man and woman in which the woman still resided as her husband had passed away. The house was solid and beautifully designed and had everything we wanted, although it did need a few updates such as replacing a oil furnace with natural gas, installing central air, revamping the kitchen layout and installing cable TV service, plus getting rid of the remote controlled antenna. We put in an offer. A few hours later our agent called and informed us that another offer was to be submitted that afternoon. I told him that we would buy it for the asking price. Our offer was accepted. So there we were, our house hadn't even been listed yet and I envisioned owning two homes at the same time. Fortunately because of the upgrades to our existing house, which we had been told was by far the nicest house on the street, it sold rather quickly. The closing dates for each didn't jive so we had to stay in a hotel for a couple of nights before taking possession. Within the next three months we had contractors upgrading our home to our liking and standards. I got a kick out of our grand kids, when before, removing the remote controlled antenna I had them go outside and watch it as I operated it to rotate. This old technology to them looked like something from outer space, Star Wars. They were in awe.

Shortly after moving to Brookfield, I received a request to do some work on the island of Antigua. Always having a problem with saying no, I was very reluctant to accept this assignment as Antigua is not one of my favorite places on earth, so I accepted under strict financial and travelling conditions. After not receiving the advanced funds by the deadline I specified I canceled the project. I received a phone call from an officer in the company promising that the funds would be deposited within three days, guaranteed. Nope, not good enough end of discussion. I was now permanently retired. Although I am not the retiring type, I had enough household projects, activities and hobbies to keep me active. I bought a new motorcycle but got bored of that after a year. I joined a golf club and played 5 days a week but got bored of that after a year. We worked out at the Y 3 times a week but got bored of that. I went back to oil painting but got bored of that after a while. Barb and I would travel to the Caribbean twice a year but got tired of that (especially the food and flights). My problem of getting bored quickly, I believe, stems from the very active, high energy and varying life I have always enjoyed. I think back quite often and reflect on the opportunities that have been handed to me or as I believe, I was directed to. From the time that my mother died, the, happenings in my life seemed almost surreal. Too me, my accomplishments were quite remarkable. To go from a high school dropout, to reporting to a Vice President of one of the largest electrical utilities in the world. To go from milking cows and plowing farm land, to crossing the Arctic Circle, the Equator, and visiting all countries in-between. To go from being an electrician, to developing and being put in charge of the Graduate Engineers in Training program.

To go from Petty Officer 2nd class in the U.S. Navy, to becoming a Commissioned Officer in the Canadian Armed Forces. To go from being an Electrical and Instrumentation Instructor, to the ranks of management. But most incredible of all was that one instant in 1968 when I gazed upon the woman who would become my wife, Barbara.

I truly believe that when being born into this world, our slate is clean. At the moment of birth that little computer in our head that we call a brain has not been pre-programmed as to our path in life. It will however, as we know, be influenced by our daily surroundings, happenings and outside influences.

Outside influences can range from human input, families, friends, suggestions, gut feelings and even enemies, to physical events, storms, flooding, earth quakes, disease and so on. One outside influence I truly believe in is spiritual. I experienced firsthand, my mom's spiritual connection as she lay dying. A little bit about my mom first.

My mom was one of those people that everyone took a liking to right from the start. She was a great mom. She was a great friend. She had a wonderful sense of humor, was totally trusting and full of love. She always talked to me as an adult and never talked down to me. Both my mom and dad loved travelling, camping and most of all they documented everything in writing, photos and films. I literally have boxes upon boxes of photos, scrap books, albums and have transferred all of our home movies to digital memory cards. My mom and dad shared strong work ethics which they instilled in me and both advanced and succeeded in their careers. My dad became a Manager of a large paper company, Domtar. My mom became a Buyer for the J.L. Hudson Company in Detroit, as a perk she had her own driver. Both were proud of their accomplishments. At the height of my mom's career, however, she developed cancer. At first she found a lump on her breast which she described as the size of a pea. She had a biopsy and I will never, ever, forget my mom's reaction when she got a phone call from the doctor informing her of the test results. Our phone was located in a hallway leading to the bedrooms and when my mom received the call, she was leaning with her back against the hallway wall. She reacted to the news by slowly sinking against the wall to the floor. It was devastating news. The tumor was cancerous. It was like receiving a death sentence. She didn't cry but she was shattered by the news and in shock. At the end of the called she handed me the phone to hang up and just sat there for a few minutes, collecting herself, which she did shortly after. Mom was strong and accepted the situation without feeling sorry for herself, outwardly anyway, and carried on as normal.

Soon after she underwent a mastectomy and had her breast removed, It wasn't long after that she had to have her other breast removed as well. The cancer was spreading and soon attacked her brain.

One evening, while visiting my mom in the hospital, she expressed concern as to what would happen to me when she died. I could not, and would not believe that my mother was going to die, and I stubbornly and naively refused to talk about it. There was no further discussion about it.

It was about mid January and the doctor had given her but a few weeks to live. My mom wanted to die at home and although mom and dad had been separated at the time, which was an amicable arrangement, my dad took a leave of absence from his work to stay home and care for her. As the brain cancer spread it started to affect my mom's behaviour. At first it was little things like calling our dog a cat. One day my mom asked me to go and get her some Tang. I had no idea what Tang was but came to learn that it was an orange drink, and had recently been developed for astronauts in the space program. I brought home the Tang but by then she didn't want it. As I previously said; I believe that we enter life with a clean slate and that there are no predetermined destinies. Our paths through life are developed as a result of a variety of physical influences or inputs from family, friends, environment, school etc; but I truly believe that there can be a spiritual influence as well. I witnessed this influence first hand as my mom slowly deteriorated. My mom was coherent and conscious of us and her surroundings in the beginning, but that began to worsen week by week until finally we and her surroundings didn't exist. With eyes closed, she started to live her life backwards, verbally. She would talk out loud about significant events in her life, starting from the present and gradually through to the past. All of her memories where in precise order of time and organized, not skipping around. The one mystery to us at the time was her constant and daily reference to April 26. Some weeks passed and my mom who was confined to the couch in the living room during this time, continued to relate to the past until she reached her childhood, all stories accurate and sensible. Late one night my dad came to my room and woke me saying its time Gary. We both knelt down beside my mom on the couch and prayed. My mom then passed peacefully away at ***one minute past midnight April 26 1963.*** That date was no longer a mystery it was a spiritual phenomenon. There is so much more to life and death than we mortals will ever know, but we can philosophize, and that is what I have done throughout my life, not in the general sense, but just to make sense of my mother's life and death.

The dictionary defines death as: The permanent cessation of all biological functions that sustain a living physical organism. The key words to me are, physical organism. The only purpose of our physical being is to transport our little, but super powerful computer contained in our head, to where it wants to go or what it wants to see, and it sees a lot, more than we can comprehend, constantly recording and storing everything. At the end of the day our computer shuts us down, we call it being tired and we go to sleep. Our computer doesn't however, it is sorting and filing and ***transmitting*** everything experienced during our day. I truly believe that these transmissions are sent to the other 'side' and stored in what we call Heaven.

I also believe that our so called dreams, represent this shuffling of data, for example, an existing file concerning a past work experience is bumped to a new position, and while being replaced and moved, we experience a confusing array of internal visions. Some of these visions can be nightmarish and terrifying, so much so, that we are not able to experience such emotions or fear, in our normal conscious state, nor can we accurately express such terror. Similarly we can experience total ecstasy and elation that we cannot experience in our normal conscience state. From personal observation of my mom's mental state during her last few subconscious weeks and days, I truly believe that she experienced the latter, and was in a spiritual contact of communication, which resulted in her knowing exactly the date of her final transfer.

April 26, 1963 was my mother's time to join others who passed on before her, her father, grandparents, acquaintances and so on. Someone from my mom's past life summoned her. It was time to move on to a loftier purpose. I believe that a tiny part of her new purpose was to tie up some lose ends that she couldn't manage before she died. She left this world with a concern as to what would happen to me. Since her passing, and for most of my adult life, I have always felt her presence, guidance and actions. The feeling of her presence is not as strong now as it has been in the past, as I believe that she has moved on to other things. Her mission accomplished. We will be together again, on the other side, and not in the so distant future. Thanks mom.

CPSIA information can be obtained
at www.ICGtesting.com
Printed in the USA
BVHW031101201020
591250BV00004B/6

9 781525 582929